Furnished Holiday Lettings

A Tax Guide

John Endacott

Furnished Holiday Lettings

A Tax Guide

John Endacott

Published by:

Claritax Books Ltd
6 Grosvenor Park Road
Chester, CH1 1QQ

admin@claritaxbooks.com

ISBN: 978-1-908545-05-3

Disclaimer

This publication is sold with the understanding that neither the publishers nor the authors, with regard to this publication, are engaged in providing legal or professional services.

The material contained in this publication does not constitute tax advice and readers are advised that they should always obtain such professional advice before acting, or refraining from acting, on any information contained in this book. Readers are also advised that UK tax law is subject to frequent and unpredictable change.

Every effort has been taken to compile the contents of this book accurately and carefully. However, neither the publisher nor the author can accept any responsibility or liability to any person, whether a purchaser of this book or not, in respect of anything done or omitted to be done by any such person in reliance, partly or wholly, on any part or on the whole of the contents of this book.

About the author

John Endacott BSc (Econ), FCA, CTA (Fellow) is a tax partner with Francis Clark LLP where he heads up a private client tax team in the Truro office specialising in advice to entrepreneurs and private clients. As part of this role John provides support to the firm's Agricultural and Rural Business and Leisure and Tourism Teams.

John offers high level tax advice combined with commercial acumen in terms of managing and advising on personal and business transactions. He also assists with tax planning in respect of capital gains tax, inheritance tax and income tax as well as with personal financial planning generally.

John is a regular writer for the tax professional press. He has written widely over the last decade (especially for Taxation, Tax Journal and Tax Adviser). He has contributed to Tolley's Tax Planning, TAXline Tax Planning, Taxwise, Tolley's Practical Tax, Finance Act handbooks and Simon's. He is also the editor of Sumption. John and his team also wrote all three editions of Tolley's Capital Gains Tax Planning. He was shortlisted for Tax Writer of the Year at the LexisNexis Taxation Awards in 2009.

John is an occasional lecturer and often gives presentations on capital gains tax. He supports the work of the Tax Faculty and is its South West Representative. He is also a member of the Tax Faculty Private Client Tax Sub-Committee. He is an examiner for the ICAEW and a former examiner of the CIOT.

Since the Budget in April 2009, John has been actively involved in advising on the proposed changes to the FHL regime and has appeared in the press and on radio and television to discuss the changes. John has been quoted in Parliament and has regularly met with officials from HM Treasury and HM Revenue & Customs to discuss taxation matters.

About the publisher

Claritax Books was launched in September 2011 to sell high quality tax books at competitive prices. The books are produced for employers, accountants, tax advisers, lawyers and other professionals. Some of the UK's best known tax authors have already written for Claritax Books, covering topics such as company cars, tax appeals, furnished holiday lettings, capital allowances, stamp duty land tax and trusts. Please visit our website at www.claritaxbooks.com to see details of all the books currently available, and of others that are coming soon.

Claritax Books is a trading name of Claritax Books Ltd (company number 07658388, VAT number 114 9371 20). Alongside the publishing business, the company operates a tax news website called Taxation Daily (www.taxationdaily.com). This free site provides a central resource for tax news developments in the UK.

Claritax Books Ltd is based in Chester, England.

Abbreviations used

CAA 2001   Capital Allowances Act 2001
CGT   Capital Gains Tax
CTA 2009   Corporation Tax Act 2009
CTA 2010   Corporation Tax Act 2010
ECJ   European Court of Justice
EU   European Union
EEA   European Economic Area
FA   Finance Act
FHLs   Furnished Holiday Lettings
HMRC   Her Majesty's Revenue & Customs
ITA 2007   Income Tax Act 2007
ITEPA 2003   Income Tax (Earnings and Pensions) Act 2003
ITTOIA 2005   Income Tax (Trading and Other Income) Act 2005
NRLS   Non-Resident Landlords Scheme
OECD   Organisation for Economic Co-operation and
                Development
SDLT   Stamp Duty Land Tax
SIPP   Self Invested Personal Pension
SSAS   Small Self Administered Scheme
TCGA 1992   Taxation of Chargeable Gains Act 1992
TOGC   Transfer of a Going Concern
TIOPA 2010   Taxation (International and other Provisions) Act
                2010
VATA 1994   Value Added Tax Act 1994

Foreword

The furore over the proposed abolition of the special furnished holiday lettings tax rules and the changes introduced by FA 2011 mean that it is timely to look in detail at these tax laws.

It is expected that users of this book will be familiar with the basics of the furnished holiday lettings rules, so the purpose of this book is to act as a reference work and as a source of detailed guidance on the more complex issues that can arise. Much of what follows concentrates on the boundary between passive investment income and trading income for tax purposes.

Hopefully, readers will find this guide useful. I also hope that there is further action by the tax authorities to deal with some of the unacceptable grey areas of the rules in the hope that this will achieve a fairer and more consistent tax system.

The tax legislation and guidance used in this book are correct as at the time of writing. The attention of readers is, however, drawn to the disclaimer on page 'v' above.

John Endacott
Francis Clark LLP
October 2011

Table of contents

1. Background to the tax rules

1.1 The growth in self-catering accommodation

After the Second World War, holiday camps were very popular as an affordable family holiday destination. They provided catered accommodation which top end hotels, guest houses and bed and breakfast establishments also offered. There was some letting of properties in holiday locations but it was fairly limited.

During the 1960s, holidays became more diverse and overseas packaged holidays became commonplace. At the same time catered holidays in the UK became more expensive as wage costs increased. These trends continued through the 1970s and UK holiday makers also came to have higher expectations of the accommodation that should be available for them. These expectations included a desire for more spacious accommodation, better standards of furnishings and heating, and better facilities.

Letting agents established themselves as middlemen between the consumers and the holiday accommodation providers. As this was before the days of the internet, seasonal catalogues were produced of the properties that were available. These became the established way of sourcing properties by holiday makers although repeat custom remained important. The letting agents imposed standards on the properties that they were prepared to let and holiday makers came to expect certain standards of the properties provided by the various agents.

So, by the late 1970s there was an established UK self-catering holiday accommodation industry which operated alongside hotels, bed and breakfasts, campsites and caravan parks. However, the UK tax rules had not kept up with the changing social trends and there was uncertainty as to the nature of the taxable income generated by such self-catering establishments. Was it trading income or rental income?

This was before self-assessment, and Inspectors of Taxes varied in the way they assessed the income and treated the expenses. Matters came to a head in 1982 with the cases of *Gittos v Barclay, Griffiths v Jackson* and *Griffiths v Pearman*.

Cases: *Gittos v Barclay (HMIT)* [1982] BTC 197; *Griffiths (HMIT) v Pearman, Griffiths (HMIT) v Jackson* [1983] BTC 68

1.2 The tax case hiatus

The *Griffiths* cases concerned the letting of student accommodation in Bristol where properties had been adapted to be let as furnished flats or bedsits to students, together with communal bathrooms and kitchens.

Justice Vinelott in the High Court held that the income was derived from the exploitation of a proprietary interest in land and was not income derived from a trade. This does not seem that surprising but it did reverse the decision of the General Commissioners (the old First-tier Tribunal level of hearing) and showed that the parameters were uncertain.

The *Gittos* case was far more significant in terms of the impact of the decision. Justice Goulding refused the appeal brought by Mr Gittos as the taxpayer. The point was, under the rules then in force, that rental income was assessable on the husband of the married couple under the joint taxation rules, without any form of personal allowance. By contrast, trading income received by a wife would have benefited from wife's earned income relief which was effectively a second personal allowance.

Justice Goulding gave the impression in his *obiter* comments that the decision was fairly close, and whilst he found against the taxpayer, holding that the income was rental income rather than trading income, this was on the basis of the facts determined by the General Commissioners. Justice Goulding asked whether the question was:

> "whether the activities of Mrs Gittos over and above the mere exploitation of her landed property were significant enough to make her a trader and not a mere landowner who derived an income by exploiting her property. It is not of course possible to give an answer to such a question in general terms. It is a question of fact and degree. I can quite see that there are forceful

arguments on both sides. Mr Gittos, in his address in reply, took the case of an hotelier, who is undoubtedly carrying on a trade, and pointed out how similar, so far as they extend, are his wife's activities in respect of Millendreath to those of an hotelier. But, of course, they do not go nearly so far or require nearly so much activity on the owner's part."

The closeness of the decision was then made clear by the fact that Justice Goulding stated that he was unable to say whether he would have come to the same conclusions on the facts as the General Commissioners had done. However the Commissioners had determined that, on the facts, the income derived by Mr and Mrs Gittos was rental income rather than trading income and he could not overturn that.

The facts that the General Commissioners had determined were that Mr and Mrs Gittos owned leases on two bungalows at Millendreath Holiday Village near Looe in Cornwall. There were 140 bungalows at the Holiday Village which also included a marina, laundrette, shop and tennis court, all of which were enjoyed by the holiday makers residing in the village. The other facilities at the site included a colour television and the provision of a cleaner and a caretaker by the landlord. The leases contained a clause restricting their use for any purpose other than that of holiday accommodation and the village was closed during the months of November, December, January and February expect for the storage of furniture. These restrictions were enforced by the landlord and it was a planning condition for the site.

It was possible for the overall landlord of Millendreath Holiday Village to deal with all bookings and servicing of the bookings and then to pay over just 75 per cent of the monies received, the landlord retaining 25 per cent. Mr and Mrs Gittos did not adopt this approach. Instead they operated a business in Mrs Gittos' name, known as "Kelletts", and that name was registered as a business under the Business Names Act 1975. There was a separate bank account for the business. Mr and Mrs Gittos lived in Gloucestershire and advertisements were placed in five newspapers in Gloucestershire each year and circulars were sent every January to former customers asking if they wished to rebook. Mrs Gittos dealt with all of the enquiries and bookings, collecting deposits and sending confirmations. It was her practice to arrange a visit for all those who had confirmed bookings.

Preparation for the holiday season involved two journeys to Cornwall by Mr and Mrs Gittos, taking blankets and house linen down to the bungalows and at the end of the season a similar amount of work was involved in clearing and cleaning the properties for the winter. At no time did Mr and Mrs Gittos occupy the holiday bungalows apart from the time spent getting them ready at the start and end of the season.

Mr and Mrs Gittos argued before the General Commissioners that the activity was an enterprise and that the nature of the trade was the promotion and sale of seaside holidays rather than the receipt of rental income. The General Commissioners had held that it was derived from the provision of furnished lettings and was not trading income.

This case is particularly significant because it did not suffer from some of the grey areas that otherwise confused the position. There was no owner occupation by Mr and Mrs Gittos; the properties could not be occupied as residential dwellings because of the planning permission restrictions; there were facilities of a very high standard and Mrs Gittos was actively involved in the activity. On this basis very few, if any, self-catering holiday accommodation businesses were ever going to qualify as trading income.

However, a large number of self-catering accommodation establishments were being treated as trades by tax inspectors. What was to be done? A sizeable hiatus followed and there was massive lobbying for a change in the tax rules to overturn the High Court decision. The uncertainty continued throughout 1983 and it became something of an election issue in some coastal towns during the general election of that year. The result was a commitment by the Conservative government to bring in special tax rules to deal with the position and these were eventually introduced in FA 1984.

Cases: *Gittos v Barclay (HMIT)* [1982] BTC 197; *Griffiths (HMIT) v Pearman, Griffiths (HMIT) v Jackson* [1983] BTC 68

1.3   The special furnished holiday lettings rules

There was considerable debate and consultation leading up to the introduction of the furnished holiday lettings (FHLs) rules in FA 1984. In the end the decision was made not to treat such income as trading income but rather to introduce rules that deemed the income to be trading income for certain tax purposes. The basis of doing this was not to adopt any subjective tests but rather to use an objective test based upon the number of days for which the property was available for letting and the number of days it was actually let. Whilst the government had originally sought higher limits, it was eventually agreed that a property would need to be available for letting for 140 days and actually let for 70 days in a year. Provisions were introduced to allow winter lets as the holiday letting season was shorter in the mid-1980s and the letting of properties at Christmas and in the autumn and spring was unusual at the time. Provisions were also introduced to allow averaging across properties where an owner let more than one holiday unit.

When introduced, the rules established that owners of FHL properties should be entitled to the offset of losses against other income as if losses generated from FHLs were losses of a trade. For capital gains tax purposes such properties were deemed to be a trade, such that rollover relief, hold-over relief and (at the time) retirement relief were all permitted. Capital allowances were available as if the activity was a trade and the income was also deemed to be net relevant earnings for pension contribution purposes.

These rules continued unchanged until the unexpected announcement in the 2009 Budget that the rules were to be abolished with effect from 6 April 2010. The reason given for the change at the time was that the FHL rules were discriminatory under EU law as they were restricted only to properties situated in the UK. This was clearly in breach of EU law and there is no doubt that the scope had to be extended. The Budget announcement provided that such rules should be immediately available to all properties within the EEA. However, there was clearly a further desire to abolish the special FHL provisions, prompted by a feeling on the part of HMRC and HM Treasury that the tax rules were being abused and that they were an unnecessary complication.

As a result of considerable lobbying, and a change in the government, the repeal of the FHL rules was not carried through but the rules were changed. FA 2011 restricted the use of losses with effect from 2011/12 and tightened the day count limits to 210 days and 105 days respectively. As a result of lobbying on the damage that these tighter day count limits may do to the self-catering accommodation industry, a new under-used property averaging relief was also introduced (commonly known as the "period of grace" provision). These measures are considered further in **Chapter 3**.

1.4 Diversity of properties

One of the issues to address when advising on tax in connection with self-catering accommodation is the diversity of owners and of the properties concerned.

The properties vary considerably in their physical nature and size and also in terms of geographical issues. Properties may have been designed and built solely for use as holiday accommodation or may just be residential accommodation that is being exploited in that way. Properties may be homes (either main or second homes) that are occupied by the family for part of the year and let to visitors for the rest. The extent of the lettings can vary considerably from a few weeks up to all year. Properties may be single unit accommodation or large complexes with swimming pools, games rooms and outside play areas.

As far as geography is concerned, the nature of the letting will vary depending on the location. This may be as a result of historical as well as local environmental factors. In areas such as the Lake District, Cotswolds and Exmoor it is easy to achieve high levels of occupancy because of the year-round local attractions, the quality of transport links and the proximity to large urban conurbations. Such properties are often popular with those looking to take part in walking or for families just interested in having large get-togethers. By contrast, other locations may be famous for a particular festival or event, such as Wimbledon or the British Grand Prix. Others still may benefit from a local event, such as Glastonbury or the Badminton Horse Trials, but may also be in areas which have the additional benefit of a good year-round tourist trade.

Properties located on the periphery of the UK tend to be popular in the high summer but overall have shorter letting seasons. Much of this is to do with transport links, travel costs and the weather. Island locations such as the Isles of Scilly or the Hebrides naturally have more restrictions and barriers to achieving high occupancy. Periods of letting can vary, with traditional one and two week holidays in England having become less common and short breaks now often the norm, typically booked online at very short notice. However, in some areas (such as parts of Scotland) it may well still be the norm to book properties by the calendar month, resulting in an entirely different pattern of occupancy. Other areas, such as Northern Ireland, do not have highly developed tourist economies, so booking seasons naturally tend to be shorter.

In all cases, local issues need to be considered. Overseas properties may be in popular tourist locations but have often been cheaply constructed for use during hot weather and may not be designed or configured for year-round occupation. There is also a great diversity of owners to consider, including farmers, bed and breakfast owners, hotels with dedicated self-catering accommodation alongside catered accommodation, campsites and caravan park owners, as well as golf courses, estate owners and unfurnished residential landlords.

The range of owners and accommodation means that it is a very diverse sector and this was apparent during the lobbying in respect of the potential tax changes. It is clear that HM Treasury and HMRC have limited information available to them concerning the sector, and the data captured from tax returns is poor. In many cases, even where the tax reliefs applying to FHLs are important to the taxpayer, the property is still not being returned as FHLs on the dedicated tax pages that would apply. It is certainly common for such properties to be incorporated within partnership pages and within the activities of other businesses. So it is incumbent upon the adviser to consider carefully the basis of any tax treatment being adopted or tax reliefs being claimed.

A further point is that whilst individual ownership is the most common in terms of number of owners, there are a large number of corporate owners and of properties owned by trustees. All of these factors need to be taken into account by the adviser.

1.5 Direct tax legislation governing furnished holiday lettings

As explained above, FA 1984 led to the introduction of specific tax legislation for the commercial letting of furnished holiday accommodation. For income tax purposes this legislation is contained within the property income rules in ITTOIA 2005, and specifically in Part 3, chapter 6, s. 322 to 328. This relates to the qualifying conditions for furnished holiday lettings; the legislation relating to loss relief is in ITA 2007.

For corporation tax purposes the main legislation is in CTA 2009, Part 4 chapter 6, s. 264 to 269, but with some aspects also contained within CTA 2010, especially as far as losses are concerned.

The capital gains tax provisions are contained in TCGA 1992 – specifically s. 241 and 241A.

For most practitioners, FHLs are far more commonly encountered as an individual's concern, rather than as a corporate affair. For this reason, the primary focus of this book tends to be upon the income tax legislation. The book addresses, in particular, the more common scenarios encountered by practitioners in day to day practice. Later chapters expand on the common scenarios where tax planning advice is routinely sought. However, it is important not to overlook the basics and to understand the basis of income taxation in terms of considering more complex planning possibilities involving capital allowances and loss relief.

1.6 The income tax rules

It is important to re-emphasise that FHLs are only a deemed trade for certain purposes. For income tax purposes, profits are assessed as property business income within ITTOIA 2005, Part 3. The furnished holiday letting rules are a chapter within that Part. This means that when it comes to considering expenses it is the property business income rules that apply. In truth, since the reform of property income in the mid-1990s, these rules are largely based upon trading principles, but the rules are not identical, and it is important to apply correct principles and to avoid incorrect assumptions.

1.7 Accounting period

The first point to remember is that the accounting period for income tax purposes can only be the physical year concerned, although accounts can be made up to 31 March rather than 5 April. This is the case as far as individuals, trustees and property business partnerships are concerned. If a trading business has FHLs, then even if that income is separately dealt with outside of the main trading activity, that income will be assessed on the accounting period of the partnership concerned.

1.8 Relief for loan financing costs

It is common for furnished holiday lettings to be purchased with debt finance and interest costs can often be one of the largest items in the property income and expenditure account.

In accordance with the normal rules (as set out in the HMRC *Property Income Manual* at paragraph 2105) interest relief is available on borrowing costs up to the value of the property when it was first let. Where there is equity in a property, by reference to the value when it was first let, this can be released by means of a further loan advance and tax relief can be obtained on that additional interest cost (see HMRC *Business Income Manual* at paragraph 45700, Example 2). Conversely, if a loan draw-down is made against equity in a property, such that it takes the borrowings in excess of the value of the property when it was first let and any subsequent capital expenditure, the interest costs must be apportioned as between the qualifying and non-qualifying amount and any non-qualifying interest disallowed.

It is therefore important to keep a record of the cost of the property when first let, which will not necessarily be the same as the cost of the property as far as capital gains tax is concerned. For instance, where a property has been used as a family holiday home and is subsequently brought into use in a property business, the relevant figure is the value at the time the property is first introduced into the property business.

Where there is owner occupation of a property, the interest expense may need adjustment for own use, in line with the normal rules for adjustments to property business expenses.

1.9 Own use adjustments

ITTOIA 2005, s. 272 provides that the standard trading computation provisions apply to expenses that are not incurred wholly and exclusively for the purposes of the property business. This rule is contained in ITTOIA 2005, s. 34. This provides that "if an expense is incurred for more than one purpose, this section does not prohibit a deduction for any identifiable part or identifiable proportion of the expense which is incurred wholly and exclusively for the purposes of the trade."

The issue here is that it is common for FHL properties to be made available to friends and family for their own use during the course of the year. In practice there tend to be two types of properties – those that are only ever used as commercial FHLs and those that are both an FHL property and a second family home. In the latter case it is important to consider very carefully the appropriate tax deductions to be made when preparing the property income and expenditure statement of the FHL business.

HMRC Helpsheet 253 states that where a property is not available for letting for part of the year, as it is closed for part of the year, the owner can still deduct the whole of the expenses for the year such as insurance, interest and utilities provided that there is no private use of the property. Where there is private use of the property then an apportionment of these expenses is required.

This apportionment is often overlooked and as such it is a common source of HMRC enquiries into FHL businesses. Even where the point is picked up the adjustments are not always as well considered as they should be. The difficulty is how to deal with the period when a property is neither let to holiday makers nor occupied by the family for their own use. The legislation requires that only the "identifiable proportion" is claimed as a deduction. Where a property is available throughout the entire year, and there is a very high level of occupation of the property by holiday makers, but there is also two weeks occupation by the family, it is probably entirely reasonable to reduce the deductible expenditure by just 2/52nds. However, where the property is not available for the entire year and there is much lower level of occupation by holiday makers and it is clear that the property has been available for the family to use at other times (should they so wish) then a much larger restriction of expenses is probably required.

The key point is to consider the appropriate adjustment fully and to ensure that it has been documented accordingly as part of the preparation of the income and expenditure account and the appropriate self-assessment tax return.

For corporate owners there are further such considerations because of the benefit in kind legislation. For overseas properties there are particular issues in this respect which are covered in **Chapter 4**. The matter is dealt with more generally in **Chapter 5**.

1.10 Jointly held property

It is possible to allocate profits or losses from a furnished holiday lettings business between a married couple or civil partners in whatever way the couple chooses (ITA 2007, s. 836). It is important to note that this is only possible where the property is jointly held in the first place; profits cannot be allocated to a wife if a property is in the sole name of a husband. In such a case it would be necessary to maintain either that the wife had her own sole trade activity or (more probably) that she was an employee (with consequent PAYE obligations on the husband).

Also, problems can arise where a property is in fact partnership property and s. 836 only applies to a property jointly held between a husband and a wife. There is flexibility as far as trading profits of a partnership are concerned in any event but care will be required if it was intended to split a business for VAT purposes.

The position of a furnished holiday lettings business needs to be distinguished from that of a normal rental business where the same flexibility to split profits and losses between a married couple does not exist. For normal rental businesses the profits or losses must be split equally for properties held under a joint tenancy, although an unequal split is possible if a property is held as tenants in common and the requirements of ITA 2007, s. 837 are complied with – including notifying HMRC within 60 days.

1.11 Non-resident owners

The Non-Resident Landlords Scheme (NRLS) is an arrangement for taxing UK rental income of persons whose "usual place of abode" is outside of the UK. The legislative provisions are contained in ITA 2007, s. 971. As FHLs are considered to be a rental income activity, non-resident owners of FHL properties are subject to the NRLS. If the activity is carried on as a trade then the NRLS does not apply.

The NRLS operates by requiring the tenant to deduct basic rate income tax from the gross rent before it is paid over to the landlord and to account for the tax so deducted to HMRC. However, where approval is first obtained from HMRC to operate the NRLS then it is permissible for the rent to be paid gross to the overseas landlord. Clearly in the case of FHL properties it is important for approval to be obtained under the scheme such that rents can be paid gross. A letting agent should be both familiar with this and able to make the necessary arrangements. However, problems can occur if no letting agent is engaged or if the owner goes abroad without advising the agent.

If the scheme does not apply, and the agent deducts the appropriate tax and pays it across to HMRC, a substantial tax refund is likely to be due to the owner because of the significant level of expenses incurred in operating a furnished holiday lettings business compared to that of a normal rental business.

1.12 Net relevant earnings

Assessable income from furnished holiday lettings is relevant income for the purposes of enabling the making of pension contributions to relevant pension schemes in accordance with FA 2004, s. 189.

Historically this benefit was of more use as under the "old" carry forward and carry back provisions this sometimes enabled pension contributions to be made in the circumstances where otherwise there would have been no net relevant earnings. However, this is less relevant today for various reasons: the facility to make a gross contribution of £3,600 each year regardless of net relevant earnings, the changes introduced by A Day on 6 April 2006, the ageing of the population and the general decline in saving through registered pension schemes. As such, this provision is not considered further in this book.

1.13 Specific tax issues to consider

A key issue to address is whether the activity is property letting or the carrying on of a trade. The distinctions are often not well appreciated and uninformed decisions are made. Furnished holiday lettings are only deemed trades for certain tax purposes and now have their own entirely separate loss relief rules that are not very attractive. Whilst treatment as a trade may well give rise to National Insurance liabilities (although not for owners over state retirement age) it may still be much more preferable to have all the benefits that go with the carrying on of a trade.

Apart from the direct tax issues that come out of the FHL rules, the other important issues for owners include:

- liability to business rates;
- liability to VAT on income;
- entitlement to business property relief for inheritance tax purposes; and
- foreign taxes and the availability of double tax relief.

These issues are all addressed later in this book.

2.   Property letting or trading?

2.1   Introduction

Following FA 2011, the question of whether or not a furnished holiday lettings activity amounts to a trade has implications for enhanced income tax loss relief options. Trading status would also support a claim for business property relief (see **Chapter 7**).

Then there are National Insurance and Working Tax Credits to consider. There are no specific FHL rules in the National Insurance legislation. Therefore it is strictly necessary to consider whether or not the activities amount to a trade in order to establish whether Class 2 and Class 4 contributions are due. Correspondence has been issued by the National Insurance Contributions Office to FHL operators in the past, asking various questions to try to establish whether or not the activities of furnished holiday lettings can amount to a trade and so be liable to National Insurance. Also, as considered further in **Chapter 8**, similar comments apply to Working Tax Credits where the test is whether the worker is self-employed.

However, it is the benefits of the income tax trading loss relief options which are now most likely to encourage FHL operators to look more closely at the correct tax law interpretation of their activities.

2.2   The legislation and badges of trade

Trade is defined as including "any venture in the nature of trade". This definition has applied since at least 1853. There is a lack of any further statutory guidance on this and so it is necessary to rely upon case law — much of which is very dated and difficult to relate to modern facts.

A body of case law built up over time in respect of whether or not an activity represented a trading activity subject to income tax. Over time, the courts and HMRC have codified these into "badges of trade" and indeed these were arrived at from a report by the Royal Commission back in 1955. A summary of badges of trade is contained in *Marson v Morton* and these are covered in the HMRC Business Income Manual at BIM20205.

In the context of income from providing holiday accommodation, the central issue is whether the income represents an investment return from the exploitation of an asset or whether the property represents a fixed asset which is the setting in which the trade is carried on. The existence of a valuable asset dwarfing the income being generated does not of itself determine that the return is a mere investment return. One only has to consider farms, hotels and care homes to realise that. It is not the asset but the nature of the income involved which is crucial.

Law: Income Tax Act 2007, s. 989

Case: *Marson v Morton and others* [1986] BTC 377

2.3   Case law prior to FA 1984

The starting point is a case concerning a charitable maternity hospital in Dublin and the letting of the Rotunda Rooms prior to the First World War.

The Rotunda Rooms were constructed in the late eighteenth century to provide an income for the hospital to cover maintenance costs, etc. The building was connected with the hospital by an internal passage and the rooms were let by the hospital charity for entertainments, concerts, cinema shows and the like. The letting periods varied from one night to up to six months and the letting price included the use of seating and heating. Further charges were made for gas and electric light based on the usage shown by the respective meters. A substantial income was derived from this activity.

The case proceeded through the Special Commissioners, the Irish High Court and then the Irish Court of Appeal until it eventually reached the House of Lords. While the Special Commissioners found that the activity amounted to a trade, the High Court and the Court of Appeal both held that the income was that from land and property. At first sight, it does seem surprising that this income could be anything other than income from land and property. However, the House of Lords held that it was income from trading.

In giving judgment, the Lord Chancellor stated that the hospital would:

"retain control of the premises, select the persons to whom the user is granted and regulate the conduct and behaviour of the persons allowed to resort thereto, and, for the purposes of enabling or facilitating the making of contract for such user, they have properly fitted up the Rotunda Rooms with fixtures, fittings and other things — some at least being clearly chattels — and provide attendance and other services."

So there are two crucial deciding points that come out of this:

1. the retention of control of the premises; and
2. the provision of services.

These are the points to look out for in establishing whether the property is being exploited in the course of a trade or whether another person is being allowed unfettered use of the property.

A decade later there was another significant case which touched on this issue. *Salisbury House Estate Limited* is a well-known case involving the owner of a large office block let to tenants as unfurnished offices. The company had no other business except the letting out and management of the one property. The company maintained a sizable staff to manage the property and undertake all the usual management services. The property consisted of 800 unfurnished rooms let out to some 200 tenants with 78 leases for periods ranging from 2 to 21 years, together with 89 tenancy agreements and 26 informal tenancies. But while the scale was large, it was still only letting income.

So in the *Salisbury House* case, although the owner was clearly in occupation of the property in terms of the common parts, it gave similarly clear property rights to the tenants for their individual offices and the services were no more than one would expect from a landlord being manager of the common areas.

In *Gittos v Barclay,* Justice Goulding stated that the central issue was whether or not the taxpayer's activities:

"were significant enough to make her a trader and not a mere landowner who derived an income by exploiting her property. It is not of course possible to give an answer to such a question in general terms. It is a question of fact and degree. I can quite see that there are forceful arguments on both sides."

At the same time as the *Gittos v Barclay* case, there was another significant case - *Griffiths v Jackson*. This was a High Court case, again from the West Country, involving the letting of furnished accommodation mainly to students in Bristol. While the General Commissioners determined that the profits derived from a trade, the High Court held that it amounted to land and property income.

Although there was a substantial level of activity involving 11 properties, there was no significant provision of other services, with these being limited to some laundry and linen services and arrangements for cleaning of rooms and gardening. Food and car hire could be provided on request.

This case does draw out the key distinction between the *Rotunda Hospital* decision and the position in *Salisbury House* (both of which were cited in the case). The taxpayers in *Griffiths v Jackson* tried to argue that their position was no different from that of an hotelier or lodging house owner and argued that their position was similar to that in the *Rotunda Hospital* case.

Justice Vinelott considered this and in particular that in the *Rotunda Hospital* case:

> "the taxpayers remained in legal occupation of the entertainment rooms and retained control over them. The income was not derived from their property in the rooms, as it would have been if they had parted with legal occupation to someone who had carried out the activities of providing the rooms for public entertainment. That was the ground on which the *Rotunda Hospital* case was distinguished in *Salisbury House Estate Ltd.*"

The Judge went on to quote Viscount Dunedin from the *Salisbury House* case referring to the fact that "the hospital was held to be in occupation of the *whole* premises" and Lord Atkin from the same case stating that "possession and occupation of the rooms remained with the [hospital]".

Cases: *The Governors of the Rotunda Hospital, Dublin, v Coman (Surveyor of Taxes)* (1918) 7 TC 517; *Salisbury House Estate Limited v Fry* (1930) 15 TC 266; *Gittos v Barclay (HMIT)* [1982] BTC 197; *Griffiths (HMIT) v Pearman, Griffiths (HMIT) v Jackson* [1983] BTC 68

2.4   Recent case law and guidance

The deemed trading position in the furnished holiday lettings rules ensured that there was no reason to litigate on the trading status. The effect of the FA 1984 rules was to give all the benefits of trading status for tax purposes without the resultant National Insurance liabilities. Further, HMRC continued to interpret the business property relief provisions for inheritance tax fairly widely (until late 2008). The result is that there has been limited case law on property related businesses (other than for inheritance tax as considered in **Chapter 7**) since *Gittos v Barclay* and *Griffiths v Jackson*.

However, there have been some disputes that have raised the issue. In particular there have been individuals who have sought to argue that a disposal of furnished lettings (not furnished holiday lettings) should qualify for business asset taper relief. There was the obviously hopeless case of *Patel v Maidment*, which is not worthy of further comment, but *Jones & Anor* is more interesting. A further recent case that touched on these issues was on the subject of old reinvestment relief in respect of self-catering accommodation attached to a seasonal hotel in Scotland. That case was *Maclean v R&C Commrs*.

In the *Maclean* case in 2006, it was determined by the Special Commissioner that the operation of the self-catering accommodation alone did not amount to a trade. This was despite the connection with an adjacent hotel which was operated by a partnership with common ownership. The Special Commissioner, Gordon Reid commented:

> "I have not found the reasoning in the authorities particularly easy to apply to the circumstances of this appeal and such principles as I have been able to extract, I have found to be of limited value and of questionable utility in the modern context of carrying on the business (to put it neutrally) of providing serviced apartments."

Commenting on the *Griffiths* case, Reid noted that the dividing line between a property business and carrying on a trade is "a narrow one" but that the "principle that income derived from the exercise of property rights properly so-called by the owner of land is not income derived from the carrying on of a trade, is embedded in tax law".

Reid stated his conclusions on the relevant case law as:

"From the authorities cited, I derive, albeit with some difficulty, the following principles.

(1) Income derived from the exercise of property rights properly so-called by the owner of land, that is to say the exploitation of the right of property and the right of occupation, is not income derived from the carrying on of a trade.

(2) Income derived by an owner from granting or limiting his rights as owner of the land in favour of others is not regarded for income tax purposes as the carrying on of a trade. Thus, income derived from the commercial letting of furnished accommodation, whether for a short or long period, is not generally regarded as income derived from carrying on a trade, even although this activity may properly be described as the carrying on of a business. Business is a wider concept than *trade*.

(3) Activities over and above the mere exploitation of heritable property or turning to profitable account the land, of which he is the owner, may be significant enough to classify a man's business as a trade. Whether the provision of services or other activities are significant enough to cross the line between land ownership and commercial enterprise in land is a question of fact and degree depending upon the nature and extent of the operations or activities concerned.

(4) However, the fact that an owner makes the visit to his land by a licensee more attractive by providing various services, eg keeping the property in a proper state and condition, will not turn exploitation of property rights into a trade.

(5) Whether income is derived from the location of the land, which is the normal manner in which property in land yields revenue, is a relevant consideration."

It is worth repeating the above in full because it does seem to be a good summary of the position. However, it does not cover the point about occupation of the land which is relevant to so many furnished holidays lettings businesses. In the subsequent case of *Mervyn Jones* (decided on 18 November 2009), the relevance of occupation of the land was acknowledged, as in their evidence, HMRC confirmed their view that "a letting business would only constitute a trade where the owner remained in occupation of the property and provided services over and above those usually provided by a landlord".

The day after the decision in *Mervyn Jones* was published, HMRC issued a Technical Note on "Withdrawing the Furnished Holiday Lettings Rules from 2010-11". Whilst this document has been superseded more generally because of the decision not to repeal the special FHL rules, it continues to be relevant as a source of reference on this issue, in particular "Chapter 3 – Property Business or Trade?". This document states that:

"The general principle is that:

- a person who is in legal occupation of the premises, retains control over them, and provides services or facilities to a third party is trading; and
- a person who allows a third party into occupation or possession of the premises for payment is carrying on a property business.

Each case will depend on its facts but it will be unusual for the provision of furnished holiday accommodation to amount to trade, or for the services provided by a landlord of furnished holiday accommodation to amount to a separate trade.

Example 1

A person provides bed and breakfast accommodation in their property. The owner lives in the property, retains control of it and provides meals to guests. The owner is carrying on a trade.

Example 2

A person owns a holiday complex which includes five cottages which are let as holiday accommodation. The cottages are let furnished and bed linen and heating are included in the cost of the rent, as is access to other facilities on the site, which include a tennis court, swimming pool and a games room. The cottages are cleaned at the beginning of each letting.

The owner deals with all booking enquiries, reservations and payments. She arranges for cleaning, laundry and maintenance of the cottages and grounds. She also provides information to visitors about local tourist attractions, restaurants etc.

The owner is carrying on a property business. The owner is generating income from the property by allowing others to use it for specified periods in return for payment. The owner is not providing services over and above those provided by a landlord."

In a further section regarding whether services provided can amount to a separate trade the document goes on to say that

"examples of services which go beyond those normally provided, and which may amount to a separate trade are:

- the regular cleaning of rooms when they are let, and not just between changes of tenant;
- the regular supply of clean linen; or
- the regular provision of meals."

The Technical Note expands on the HMRC view expressed in *Mervyn Jones*, but is actually of fairly limited practical application because Example 1 is obvious and Example 2 does not state whether the owner is in occupation of the property or not. The final sentence of Example 2 could be interpreted as meaning that the services are insufficient to turn the activity into a trade or not regardless of whether the owner is in occupation. However, if so then there is no case law support given for that view. All Example 2 really does is to restate *Gittos v Barclay*. If the owner lived on the site (which is normal for such complexes) then it seems far more reasonable that the activity amounts to a trade. Reference should be made to the comments on *Gittos v Barclay* in **Chapter 1**. The judicial comment suggested that the services provided in the case were close to the boundary with a trading business, so occupation probably is enough to make it a trade.

Equally, the limitation of Example 1 is that it deals with the traditional bed and breakfast business rather than more modern budget hotels or surf lodges. In various discussions with HMRC during the consultation, the view continued to be expressed that hotels that do not provide food or any other significant services (such as purpose built budget hotels where the food is normally provided by another business) continue to qualify as trades because the owner is in occupation. The threshold for additional services is a very low one, it seems. If so, then if the owner is in occupation in Example 2 it should be taxed as a trade.

The further point on which the Technical Note was silent was the meaning of occupation. Does this have to be part of the same building? That seems unlikely. But what nexus must there be? An historical connection is probably helpful but it probably comes down to whether the holidaymakers viewed the owners as being resident at the location. In this context it is important to note that the owners do not have to be physically present themselves to be in occupation. An employee residing on site is sufficient – in the same way as it is for an hotel trade.

Therefore, it seems reasonable to conclude that many furnished holiday lettings complex owners are more correctly liable to taxation on the basis that they are carrying on a trade, with the resultant income tax loss reliefs and improved business property relief status that go with that conclusion.

When the special FHL rules were being abolished, HMRC seemed more sympathetic to the request for more guidance on their view as to the boundary between carrying on a trade and a property business. Subsequent to this, and with the change in stance on retaining the modified rules, the government has been less sympathetic to such requests. In the Finance Bill 2011 Committee debate David Gauke was asked to comment on the boundary between carrying on a trade and a property business and in particular whether or not it made a difference if the proprietor was in occupation on the basis of existing case law. Further guidance on this distinction was also requested from HMRC. In response all David Gauke said was that "if the proprietor provides significant services – for example, meals – the business may be a trade, in which case it would enjoy all the trade tax benefits. The status of the business will depend on the individual facts of the case".

Frankly, this isn't much help. Nor is there any official guidance in Helpsheet 253 on furnished holiday lettings. However, the point remains that for many operators it is now necessary to consider the distinction between carrying on a trade or a property business much more carefully than was the case prior to FA 2011.

Cases: *Gittos v Barclay (HMIT)* [1982] BTC 197; *Griffiths (HMIT) v Pearman, Griffiths (HMIT) v Jackson* [1983] BTC 68; *Patel v Maidment* (2003) Sp C 384; *Maclean v R&C Commrs* (2007) Sp C 594; *Jones & Anor* [2009] UKFTT 312 (TC)

2.5   Income tax trading loss reliefs

If the furnished holiday lettings business is assessable as a trade, the full range of income tax loss relief provisions will become available to it. There is nothing specific to FHLs in the income tax trading loss provisions but it is still worth making a few relevant comments. The available loss relief options would also be increased for corporation tax purposes, but as will be apparent from the following comments there is less that is worthy of note in that context.

The FA 2011 changes to the FHL rules sought to restrict income tax loss relief against other income as the previous rules were seen as over-generous in that context, and open to abuse. One particular point that tended to come up on the "old" loss relief regime was the restrictions in ITA 2007, s. 74C for non-active individuals and in ITA 2007, s. 103B for non-active partners. These sections require the individual concerned to spend at least 10 hours a week actively involved in the activities of the trade, failing which the available loss relief is capped at £25,000. In the past this restriction has most commonly arisen on a first year loss claim where there has been substantial property refurbishment and a claim on integral features (see **Chapter 5**). In such cases, if the individual did not live close to the property, and if a letting agent was instructed, then it was unlikely that the individual was actively involved on average for more than 10 hours a week. Going forward, it is unlikely that trading status will be achieved for a sole trader in such circumstances but it is possible that the non-active partner restriction could still bite. Therefore, if trading status is considered appropriate, and if the aim is to achieve a very large loss for a very high earner who is not involved on a day to day basis, then this restriction is likely to apply. Due consideration to the matter will then need to be given.

It is also necessary to consider whether a loss is commercial. At first sight this may not be considered to be much of an issue, especially as even for property business status it is a requirement that the activities be carried on on a commercial basis (see **Chapter 3**). However, there is a more restrictive definition of a commercial loss for the purposes of early trade loss relief (ITA 2007, s. 72) than for sideways loss relief (ITA 2007, s. 64).

For sideways loss relief it is only necessary to satisfy ITA 2007, s. 66(3) which says:

> "If at any time a trade is carried on so as to afford a reasonable expectation of profit, it is treated as carried on at that time with a view to the realisation of profits".

In contrast ITA 2007, s. 74(2)(b) says that the trade must be carried on:

> "in such a way that profits of the trade could reasonably be expected to be made in the basis period or within a reasonable time afterwards".

The test for early trade loss relief is much tougher and requires profits to be expected sooner. Therefore, where a loss arises due to very high borrowing costs, and this position is expected to continue, it is unlikely that early trade loss relief will be available and a claim for sideways loss relief should be made instead. This point was considered in the furnished holiday lettings case of *Brown v Richardson*.

Case: *Brown v Richardson* (1997) Sp C 129

3. Meeting the qualifying criteria

3.1 The FA 1984 rules

Despite the announcement in April 2009 that the furnished holiday lettings rules were to be abolished, that was not the eventual outcome. Indeed, the FA 2011 reform of the rules largely adds to the original FA 1984 legislative provisions as rewritten into ITTOIA 2005 and CTA 2009. The policy background to the FA 1984 provisions is considered in **Chapter 1**. In this chapter, it is sensible to start by analysing the original legislative provisions in more detail.

The provisions were originally introduced by FA 1984, s. 50 and Sch. 11. The proposed legislation was considered by the Finance Bill Committee on 5 June 1984 and at the Report stage on 11 July 1984. However, a particular difficulty here is that despite the fact that the legislation had been under discussion for some time prior to the publication of the Finance Bill, there was a substantial rewriting of the rules between the Finance Bill 1984 Committee debate and the Report stage. Therefore, whilst the commentary in the Finance Bill Committee debate is relevant, some parts of it had already been superseded by the time that the final rules were approved. There was unfortunately little new debate at the Report stage other than in connection with capital transfer tax (now inheritance tax).

In the original Committee debate, Sir William Clark had tried to have the legislation extended to capital transfer tax but was unsuccessful. The Chief Secretary to the Treasury, Peter Rees, made clear that the intention of the new legislation was only "to relieve the position, which was thought to have been disturbed by two cases recently heard in the High Court. One is called *Gittos v Barclay* and the other *Griffiths v Jackson*". As such the FHL rules have no relevance when considering business property relief for inheritance tax purposes. The implications of this are considered further in **Chapter 7**. However, it was acknowledged at the time that those businesses taxable as trades should benefit from inheritance tax relief. It is also a consistent theme throughout the Finance Bill Committee debate that the intention of the legislation was only to correct the position that had been disturbed by the court rulings.

Peter Rees also made it clear that the FHL rules apply to caravan parks – unless those caravan parks are in fact taxed as trades. In this context it is worth highlighting that the legislation applies to the "commercial letting of furnished holiday accommodation". There is no specification to restrict the definition of holiday accommodation in the legislation, which must therefore take its usual day to day meaning. The term holiday accommodation therefore goes much wider than holiday cottages.

One other theme that runs through the Finance Bill Committee debate is the concern that any beneficial tax treatment should not be exploited by second home owners. It is certainly clear that the rules go further than many MPs anticipated at the time. However, in any interpretation of the legislation it is important to keep this point in mind.

3.2 The essential requirements

3.2.1 Overview

In order to qualify as a furnished holiday letting, as opposed to the mere letting of furnished accommodation, there are two criteria that have to be satisfied:

1. the property must be let on a commercial basis with a view to the realisation of profits (ITTOIA 2005, s. 323(2)); and
2. it must meet the relevant qualifying criteria (s. 325).

As mentioned above, the property must be furnished in order to qualify (s. 323(3)(a)). The furniture and furnishings must be provided with the property and must be sufficient to enable the property to be occupied as holiday accommodation.

The references given above are for income tax purposes. The legislation for corporation tax purposes is virtually identical with the relevant provisions being CTA 2009, s. 265 and 267.

3.2.2   Rules applying from April 2012

From April 2012, the qualifying criteria in the second leg of the definition require that:

- the property is available for letting for at least 210 days (30 weeks);
- is commercially let to members of the public for at least 105 days (15 weeks).

There is also a restriction to prevent continuous occupation for a period exceeding five months (155 day test). To achieve that the property must not be occupied for more than 31 days by the same person in any period of 7 months. This restriction is designed to allow a longer let of a property out of season, although this has become much less common since the rules were first introduced as the summer letting season has extended. Letting at high rates in the half-term weeks of the autumn and spring terms, and at Christmas and New Year, has also become much more achievable.

Specifically, there are three separate day count conditions set out in ITTOIA 2005, s. 325 and CTA 2009, s. 267. All three conditions must be satisfied if a letting is to qualify:

The availability condition – "during the relevant period, the accommodation must be available for commercial letting as holiday accommodation to the public generally for at least 210 days."

The letting condition – "during the relevant period, the accommodation must be commercially let as holiday accommodation to members of the public for at least 105 days."

The pattern of occupation condition – "during the relevant period, not more than 155 days fall during periods of longer-term occupation."

3.2.3   Rules applying before April 2012

Prior to FA 2011, the day count conditions were that a property had to be available for 140 days and actually let for 70 days. The FA 2011 day count limits apply for income tax from 6 April 2012 and for corporation tax purposes for accounting periods which begin on, or after, 1 April 2012. The historic FA 1984 day count limits continue to apply for 2011/12 for both income tax and corporation tax with the benefit of a further extension as a result of the period of grace provision in ITTOIA 2005, s. 326A and CTA 2009, s. 268A. This is considered further below.

3.2.4 Practicalities

It is important to appreciate that in order to qualify as FHL, a property must be available for at least 210 days in a period. There is a concern that planning restrictions could prevent a property from being available for this minimum period of time. For instance, there can be a planning restriction that limits letting of the property to only the period between Easter and September. This would prevent qualification and neither the averaging nor period of grace elections can be used in such circumstances. This point was raised with HMRC during the consultation on the FA 2011 changes but no additional concessions were introduced. There was an implication that HMRC would be sympathetic to such a circumstance but in the post-Wilkinson world, with no ability by HMRC to issue concessions, there is simply no scope for HMRC to give a relaxation in such a scenario.

3.2.5 Period of longer-term occupation

A "period of longer-term occupation" is a continuous period of more than 31 days during which the accommodation is in the same occupation (otherwise than because of circumstances that are not normal). The word "normal" in the definition of a "period of longer-term occupation" takes its ordinary everyday meaning, so it may be construed as meaning "regular" or "usual". It is to ensure that FHL status is not denied due to exceptional and unforeseen circumstances. HMRC guidance is that it should be interpreted, as meaning the intended lettings rather than the actual lettings that take place.

Exceptional circumstances where a letting might exceed 31 days and yet still qualify as a furnished holiday letting could include a holiday maker who falls ill or has an accident, and so cannot vacate the accommodation on time. For island locations, the inability to cross back to the mainland is another possibility. There might also be exceptional instances where holiday visitors unexpectedly require a longer vacation. Qualifying lettings exceeding 31 days should, however, be the exception rather than the rule, so HMRC will review such claims critically.

A property that is owner-occupied for part of the year cannot be regarded as available for letting while it is owner-occupied. Nevertheless, the words "in the same occupation" in the definition of a "period of longer-term occupation" should be interpreted as "let in the same occupation" and do not preclude relief to an owner who moves out of his home during the holiday season and returns to live there when the season is over.

3.2.6   *HMRC guidelines and practice*

There is HMRC guidance contained in self-assessment helpsheet HS 253 and the Property Income Manual from paragraph PIM 4100 onwards. This guidance confirms that in calculating taxable income for a furnished holiday letting business the normal rules for a property business are used but FHLs must be assessed separately from any other property business profits. Further, UK and EEA businesses must be kept separate. All the furnished holiday lettings by a particular person or partnership are treated as one business. Once a particular property qualifies, all the income from that property for that year qualifies as income from the letting of FHL accommodation. It remains property income for income tax purposes so that no liability to National Insurance arises on the activity.

Where a property is kept solely for letting as FHL accommodation, but is in fact closed for part of the year, all the expenses (such as insurance, interest, etc.) for the year are an allowable deduction as long as there is no private use. Where only part of a property is let as FHL accommodation, income and expenditure should be apportioned on a just and reasonable basis.

Prior to the FA 2011 changes the HMRC guidance provided that:

> "Strictly, if a property qualifies in one tax year but does not do so in the next, the disposal value of plant and machinery should be brought into account. If income from a property temporarily ceases to qualify solely because not all the tests are satisfied for that year, capital allowances may be continued. But if a property is let on a long-term basis, or sold, or otherwise seems unlikely

to qualify in the foreseeable future, a disposal value should be brought into account."

It is to try and overcome this problem that the period of grace provision has been introduced, though it is not clear whether this concession would still apply if that fails to deal with the situation. The government and HMRC are hopeful that the period of grace provision will deal with the issue but in reality, this is a practical relaxation of the strict position and HMRC may well accept this approach on an ongoing basis in certain cases.

3.2.7   No election for FHL treatment

It is important to note that there is no question of electing for FHL treatment. It applies as a matter of fact. It is not possible to be taxed as a normal property business instead. During the consultation on the FA 2011 changes, it was requested that for ease of compliance, it should be possible to elect out of the FHL treatment. This was not accepted and so if the special treatment is not desired then it is necessary to ensure that the qualifying tests are not met.

3.2.8   Capital allowances

If plant and machinery, on which capital allowances are claimed, is partly used for private purposes then only an appropriate fraction of the capital allowances are allowed. This is the same as for any other capital allowances claim where there is private use.

3.3   Meaning of commercial letting

Regardless of the need to achieve the qualifying day count limits as set out by the legislation, there is a first stage test that the letting must be commercial. The meaning of commercial letting of furnished holiday accommodation is defined in ITTOIA 2005, s. 323 for income tax purposes and CTA 2009, s. 265 for corporation tax purposes. The wording in each case is virtually identical. The requirement is that the letting must be commercial and with a view to the realisation of profits.

The need for the accommodation to be let on a commercial basis is important, but does not always appear to be appreciated, particularly by unrepresented taxpayers. A loss in the first year of letting a property is quite usual (because of capital investment costs and lower occupancy and tariff rates) and it may be that losses occur in the second and possibly third year of a letting. However, if losses are incurred for more than three consecutive years, then it is hard to see how the letting is going to be justified as being commercial (although HMRC have tended to allow a longer period). Lettings to family and friends at reduced rates are not commercial. It is also likely to be harder to meet this test if there are very high borrowings on a property and if staff are employed to deal with all cleaning and changeovers etc. Fundamentally, if the purpose of the acquisition of the property is for someone to acquire a holiday home for themselves, then it is going to be hard to meet the requirements in s. 323.

The restriction of loss relief in the FA 2011 changes makes it clear that the government is concerned over possible abuse of the FHL regime. However, HMRC challenges to loss relief claims on grounds of lack of commerciality were very rare – surprisingly so. As explained elsewhere in this book, the ability to use losses has been severely restricted such that the issue of commerciality is now less of a concern. However, the requirement is still in the legislation and needs to be considered in each case.

A letting that makes a loss every year, or that is not forecast to show a profit for many years, is unlikely to be commercial. As already mentioned, a rule of thumb is that three consecutive years of losses are probably not commercial. In any case where losses are made, the tax return should disclose the reasons for the loss in sufficient detail to justify the claim that the activity is being carried on on a commercial basis. Proper supporting documentation should also be kept.

It is not necessary that each individual letting has to show a profit by reference to all the costs (fixed and variable). A letting that produces a contribution towards fixed costs is still commercial if that is the best that can be achieved in the circumstances. Therefore discounted last minute bookings or a close season let at a low rent are still commercial if overall the business is expected to show a profit for the year, or as part of building up the business for the future.

Whether a letting of accommodation is on a commercial basis with a view to the realisation of profits, within ITTOIA 2005, s. 323(2) and CTA 2009, s. 265(2), was considered in the Special Commissioners case of *Brown v Richardson*.

Mr Brown was a chartered accountant from Bath. In April 1992, he applied for a mortgage of up to £275,000. Part of this sum was to be applied in repaying an existing mortgage on his main residence (£65,000) and the remainder, secured on his main residence, was to be available to enable him "to purchase a holiday home". Having visited about a dozen possible houses in Cornwall he found a suitable house, which was Heather Croft, a "detached individual dormer bungalow", comprising three double bedrooms, built some 25 years earlier. The property was in the process of refurbishment. The taxpayer offered £110,000 in August 1992, which was accepted, and completion took place in October 1992.

The Special Commissioner did not accept that the letting was commercial just because Mr Brown made a taxable profit under what was then Schedule D Case VI. He held that "profits" means "commercial profits" as distinct from "profits or gains" which may be charged to tax under a particular Schedule or Case in a Schedule. It was held that the test as to whether Mr Brown had let the property "with a view to the realisation of profits" was subjective. Holiday letting had not been declared on the mortgage application form as the predominant or most significant reason for the acquisition. Moreover, Mr Brown and his family had occupied the house for three weeks in 1993 and 1994 in July to August which were the most expensive letting weeks to reserve for his own use. Mr Brown had primarily bought the property for the purpose expressed in the mortgage application, as a holiday home. He had also intended to let it as furnished holiday accommodation when he did not require it, but whilst such letting had been commercial, it had been effected with a view to generating revenue to offset costs rather than with a view to the realisation of profits. The Special Commissioner, D A Shirley said that:

> "It is plain that the lettings which took place were not uncommercial. The taxpayer engaged a competent agent who provided commercial advice and management. There is no suggestion that the charges made to tenants were uncommercial.

The number of letting days in 1993–94 and the two succeeding years was well in excess of the minimum 70 days."

But whilst the letting was commercial, it was also necessary to satisfy the second leg of the requirement by showing that Heather Croft was let "with a view to the realisation of profits". The Special Commissioner concluded that:

"This test is subjective. Looking at the accounts for 1993–94 to 1995–96, interest charges run at £9,908, £9,757, £9,603. There is a slight fall. Rents are £4,220, £4,154, £5,790. There is an increase. In his mind the taxpayer had thought at the outset that interest rates might fall and rents increase. The taxpayer made no formal projections. If one excludes interest, modest profits occur. .... The contemporary written evidence at the time the taxpayer applied for a mortgage is that he desired to purchase a holiday home. He had mixed motives for the purchase. It would be a good capital investment as he thought the market was at its bottom. It was a good opportunity. Holiday letting, of which he himself had had experience, would or could provide revenue to offset running costs. In evidence he said that holiday letting was the predominant or most significant reason for the acquisition which, if true, one might have expected to see declared on the mortgage application form. He and his family occupied the house for three weeks in 1993 and 1994 in July to August which were the most expensive letting weeks to reserve for his own use ....

I take the view that the appellant bought Heather Croft for the purpose expressed in the mortgage application, as a holiday home. That was the primary purpose. He also intended to let it as furnished holiday accommodation when he did not require it. Such letting was commercial. It was effected, however, with a view to generating revenue to offset costs rather than with a view to the realisation of profits."

Therefore, the conclusion of the case was that whilst the lettings were commercial, the property had not been purchased with a view to the realisation of profits. The property concerned was therefore not qualifying furnished holiday accommodation. Following the decision, HMRC issued RI 175 which states:

"Cases of this kind turn on their own particular facts. In this one, there was evidence on which the Special Commissioner could come to his decision. But the decision supports our view that—

- 'profits' in [ITTOIA 2005, s. 323 or CTA 2009, s. 265] means the 'commercial' and not the 'tax adjusted' profit;
- a taxpayer's expressed intentions are not necessarily conclusive. There may be evidence which points to a motive other than the income profit motive (such as a holiday or retirement home, or a long term capital profit on the disposal of the property);
- where there is evidence to suggest that a property or caravan was acquired primarily as a holiday or second home, the letting activity is likely to be carried on with a view to generating income to offset costs rather than with a view to the realisation of profits. This principle may apply equally to claims for losses incurred in some trading activities such as farming and other activities where there may be non-commercial considerations;
- claimants may fail the test in [ITTOIA 2005, s. 323 or CTA 2009, s. 265] where, as in *Brown v Richardson*, the size of the mortgage used to purchase the property or caravan is so large that the projected profitability is jeopardised or the commercial credibility of the scheme as a whole is, consequently, questionable even though individual lettings are on a commercial basis.

In these cases, we would expect a written business plan to be prepared at the outset as was so in the earlier Special Commissioners case of *Walls v Livesey*. The figures in such a plan must be credible. In *Brown v Richardson*, the taxpayer made no formal projections of the expected income but said he had made projections which (as an accountant) he was able to carry in his head.

However, his projections did not take into account inflation or contingent expenses and showed a fall in general expenses after excluding agents commission."

RI 175 goes on to deal with the further requirements that are in the opening year loss rules in ITA 2007, s. 74, but this restriction on the commerciality of the arrangements no longer directly applies, as that loss relief provision is no longer available to furnished holiday lettings following the FA 2011 changes. However, this issue is still relevant to the letting of holiday accommodation where it is taxed as a trade and this point is considered further in **Chapter 2**.

Cases: *Walls v Livesey* (1995) Sp C 4; *Brown v Richardson* (1997) Sp C 129

3.4 The relevant period

For income tax purposes, the relevant period for accommodation let by a person in a tax year for which the qualifying criteria are to be considered is set out in ITTOIA 2005, s. 324. The "relevant period" is determined as follows:

- If the accommodation was not let by the person as furnished accommodation in the previous tax year, "the relevant period" is 12 months beginning with the first day in the tax year on which it is let by the person as furnished accommodation.
- If the accommodation was let by the person as furnished accommodation in the previous tax year, but is not let by the person as furnished accommodation in the following tax year, "the relevant period" is 12 months ending with the last day in the tax year on which it is let by the person as furnished accommodation.
- Otherwise "the relevant period" is the tax year.

So, in a continuing period of letting of furnished holiday accommodation, the relevant period is the tax year. In the first year of letting, it is 12 months from commencement and in the final year of letting it is the 12 months ending with the cessation of the business.

The position for corporation tax is set out in CTA 2009, s. 266 and is slightly more straightforward as it is by reference to accounting periods. However, it is always a 12 month period that is considered. For a new source, it is 12 months from the first day in the accounting period in which the property is let. Otherwise it is usually the 12 month period ending with the last day of the accounting period.

There is then the question as to what "let by the person" means in ITTOIA 2005, s. 324 (CTA 2009, s. 266 uses the term "let by the company"). The old Inland Revenue booklet IR150 interpreted this as meaning "date of first letting" and "date of last letting" respectively. However, this has always seemed a perverse interpretation by reference to the normal rules for trading businesses and the relevant case law. The current guidance is contained in the HMRC Property Income Manual at 4112 which now uses both the IR150 terminology but also the terms "when letting began" and "date letting ceased".

The case of *Brown v Richardson* is also relevant in terms of considering the date of commencement of a furnished holiday lettings activity. The Special Commissioner made observations on the date that the activity in that case commenced, specifically:

> "The accounts for 5 April 1993 provide some indication that business had commenced. There are printing and advertising expenses and deposits received. The main holiday season starts in April but it is an agreed fact that the house was available for letting from 2 January 1993 though no letting took place until 21 May 1993. Advertising leaflets were despatched in January or February. The earliest date for business to commence would be 2 January 1993 .... Having regard to the nature of the business, I would not accept that business commenced only when the first letting occurred on 21 May 1993. A young barrister does not commence to practice only when he receives his first set of instructions for which he may have had to wait for some time."

The HMRC Property Income Manual states at 2505:

> "The date a rental business begins is a question of fact that depends on the nature of the rental business. Normally a rental business will begin when the taxpayer first enters into a transaction that exploits their land or property in a way which gives rise to a receipt of some kind.

> Where the rental business is letting property, the business can't begin until the first property is let. You need to distinguish between activities that are preparatory to letting and those business activities that are part of letting."

If expenditure is incurred prior to the commencement of the business, then it is treated like pre-trading expenditure and is deductible on the first day on which the property business is carried on. While the HMRC guidance is clear in respect of long-term letting, it is more difficult to apply it to furnished holiday lettings. What amounts to a transaction to exploit the land and property?

Example – New Business

Alice acquires a cottage in Lymington on 5 January 2012. She wants to use the property as a holiday let. She has a business plan to do so and has secured a business loan for the purchase.

Alice redecorates the property (which takes about 4 weeks) and starts to advertise it. Bookings are secured and deposits are received for holidaymakers coming to stay in the summer months. During the period of redecoration, the property is also furnished. The first guest arrives on 26 March 2012 on a last minute booking and stays for 4 nights. The HMRC guidance implies that section 324 must be read as looking at the 12 month period from 26 March 2012. This works as long as it is accepted that the furnished holiday letting commenced in 2011/12 – possibly from 5 January or at least when the redecoration is completed.

In this example, there is little to dispute because there was a letting (actual occupation) in 2011/12. But what if that booking had not been secured? Does "let" in s. 324 mean taking up occupation or the payment of a deposit? A better view is surely to interpret "let" as meaning the date of the commencement of the letting of furnished holiday accommodation in accordance with normal trading and business principles.

The best advice must always be to secure actual occupation in the tax year of acquisition (in the example above in 2011/12). Otherwise, there could be doubt as to the status of the property letting in that tax year which is relevant for loss relief (although less so after 5 April 2011), for entitlement to capital allowances and for roll-over relief purposes.

The HMRC Property Income Manual at 2510 confirms that the date of cessation of a rental business is a question of fact. However, the guidance in respect of a normal property business in this paragraph is in fact more generous than the position for furnished holidays lettings. Therefore it is quite possible (and indeed very likely) that a property business could cease to meet the requirements of the special tax rules for furnished holiday lettings but still continue as a property rental business. Hence the need for the period of grace election in ITTOIA 2005, s. 326A and CTA 2009, s. 268A and the introduction of CAA 2001, s. 13B for capital allowances purposes.

Case: *Brown v Richardson* (1997) Sp C 129

3.5 Occupancy levels

The pattern of occupation of holiday accommodation varies around the country. Whilst all year round occupation may be achievable in the Lake District, it isn't possible in many more peripheral locations. There also needs to be some allowance for lower occupancy levels in the first year of a letting and the potential for a bad summer in a business that is ultimately weather related. However, the rules do allow for averaging of occupation across multiple units and include special measures to deal with the calculation of the qualifying criteria in opening and closing years.

Part of the intention behind the FA 2011 changes was that the government felt that the regime should only be available to commercially let properties, and the definition of what constitutes commercial letting had changed since the regime was first introduced in 1984. David Gauke emphasised this point in the Finance Bill 2011 Committee debate when he said that in order to make the extension of the relief to the EEA affordable, "changes to the legislation are being made to target the tax allowances at businesses run on a truly commercial basis". As a result, it is necessary from April 2012 onwards to have a property available for letting for 210 days a year and actually let for 105 days a year, rather than the previous FA 1984 limits of 140 and 70 days respectively.

The danger in increasing the day count limits is that more remote locations within the UK are disadvantaged. So new "period of grace" rules were introduced to overcome these concerns. These concerns were acknowledged by David Gauke when he said that "it may be more difficult for certain outlying areas to meet the tests every year, but the new period of grace should go a long way to help those businesses meet the tests".

3.6   Averaging

The taxpayer may have more than one unit of accommodation let for holiday purposes. If so, it isn't necessary for each unit to have actually been let for at least 105 days, provided each unit satisfies the 210 day rule for availability and the 155 day rule for long term occupancy. In such circumstances the taxpayer may claim averaging treatment in order to satisfy the 105 day rule.

Where a person has a number of furnished holiday lettings units, some of which are individually let for less than 105 days, the landlord may apply the letting condition to the average rate of occupancy of the units. However, each unit must separately satisfy the availability condition and the pattern of occupation condition. It is necessary to make an election for averaging treatment which has a time limit of 31 January following the year of assessment.

Example – Averaging

Ollie lets five units in a holiday accommodation complex. In 2012/13 each unit is available for the entire year so that there is no doubt that the necessary conditions are satisfied.

The actual letting periods are:

	Days
Unit 1	150
Unit 2	120
Unit 3	105
Unit 4	50
Unit 5	110
Total	**535**
Average 535/5 =	107

By averaging, all five units at the complex qualify, whereas without averaging, Unit 4 would not qualify. However, it is important to note that the averaging treatment has to be claimed – a point that is often overlooked.

The logic of the averaging provision is that complexes will often consist of units of which some are more desirable than others. It is reasonable to allow guests to have a free choice of available units throughout the year. Otherwise an owner would have to insist that a guest occupied an under-used property to meet the qualifying criteria even though this may be commercially undesirable.

Law: ITTOIA 2005, s. 326; CTA 2009, s. 268

3.7   Period of grace

The main result of the lobbying and consultation on the change of the rules was the introduction of a "period of grace" provision in FA 2011. This again takes the form of an election. The relevant legislation is entitled (for both income tax and corporation tax purposes) "Under-used holiday accommodation: letting condition not met". This provides for an election for the furnished holiday lettings rules to continue to apply even though the actual letting day count condition is not met. In practice this is likely to be referred to as a "period of grace election".

This election can only apply where there is a genuine intention to let the property and the property must certainly be made available for the 210 day period. It is necessary to show that active steps were being taken to let the property, including advertising and marketing of it, and that the property was not in reality being used in another way (e.g. as a holiday home). The intention of this provision is to deal with situations such as the foot and mouth outbreak, economic downturns and the timing of Easter (such that it is possible to have two Easter breaks in one tax year and none the following year).

The HMRC guidance in HS253 confirms that the averaging election is considered to apply to a unit of accommodation in priority to considering the period of grace provision. This is by virtue of subsection 6 of the newer legislation. Therefore if a unit of accommodation only qualifies in 2013/14 by virtue of an averaging election, it can then qualify for a further two tax years (2014/15 and 2015/16) by virtue of the period of grace election. It is not possible to make both a period of grace election and an averaging election in respect of the same tax year. In the context of both the averaging provision and the period of grace provision, accommodation is read as meaning each individual unit. This gives maximum scope for holiday accommodation to continue to qualify despite an insufficiency of actual letting time.

Example – period of grace

Rosie has a holiday letting property in a remote location. She is concerned about the change in the rules as whilst she can always achieve more than 70 days, it is difficult to achieve 105 days at the property.

In 2011/12 the property achieves 77 days and so qualifies. By virtue of the period of grace it will definitely continue to qualify in 2012/13 and 2013/14. Therefore Rosie needs to achieve at least 105 days of actual letting at the property in one of the tax years 2012/13 through to 2014/15.

In summary, the period of grace requirement means that a property must meet the actual letting requirement as a minimum in at least one tax year out of every three tax years, and that this can be achieved by means of an averaging election.

In the Finance Bill 2011 Committee debate David Gauke said that:

"the period of grace is designed to help businesses that fail to meet the occupancy threshold for up to two years. Therefore, the business needs to meet the thresholds for only one year, not three. The introduction of the increased thresholds has been delayed by a year to allow businesses to adapt their letting strategies. Those should be particularly helpful to regions where the new rules may be more challenging".

Law: ITTOIA 2005, s. 326A; CTA 2009, s. 268A

3.8   Relief for losses

For income tax loss relief purposes ITA 2007, s. 127 is amended to restrict certain forms of loss relief. Previously the section deemed qualifying furnished holiday lettings to be a trade for income tax loss relief purposes apart from one minor exception. Therefore, for all practical purposes, a loss arising on furnished holiday lettings was just the same as a trading loss. That is no longer the case as ITA 2007, part 4, chapter 2 (trade losses) now applies as if ITA 2007, s. 64 - 82 and 89 - 95 are omitted. Given that chapter 2 starts with s. 60 and ends with s. 101, this does not leave much. Sections 96 - 101 deal with post cessation relief and s. 60 – s. 63 are introductory. That leaves s. 83 – s. 88, which deal with the carrying forward of losses. All that can now be done with a loss on a furnished holiday lettings business is to carry it forward against future profits of the same business.

For corporation tax purposes, loss relief in CTA 2010, part 4, chapter 2 is similarly restricted by virtue of CTA 2010, s. 65 and 67A. It applies to FHLs as if s. 37 to 44 and 48 to 54 were omitted. Given that CTA 2010, part 4, chapter 2 only consists of s. 36 to s. 54 in total, all that is left to apply is s. 36, which is introductory, and s. 45 to s. 47. Effectively all that is left is a carry forward loss relief provision.

For both income tax and corporation tax purposes, it is necessary to treat the UK and EEA as separate trades, and losses are dealt with entirely separately. In each case the losses are carried forward against future profits from the same furnished holiday lettings activity.

There is an easy trap to fall into here in that despite the fact that a furnished holiday lettings activity is a property business, a loss cannot be offset against a normal property business profit. Therefore for a client with a substantial property business, planning to incur significant expenditure on an FHL property, it may be better to have that property not qualifying as an FHL property, so that the loss arising can be used against the existing property business profit. This is likely to be particularly important to consider when a property is first acquired, as it may be better to let the property long term whilst refurbishment expenditure is incurred. Indeed, for corporation tax, a normal UK property business opens up even more loss relief possibilities as offset against total profits under CTA 2010, s. 62(3) applies.

3.9   Approach to preparation of accounts and tax returns

It is essential for those preparing FHL accounts and tax returns to understand the qualifying criteria before starting work. The detail of the rules is surprisingly poorly understood and the danger is that time is wasted unnecessarily. The qualifying criteria can have a bearing on how capital expenditure is relieved, on the split of income between a married couple or civil partners, on how losses are utilised and on whether averaging or period of grace elections are required. The issue can also be very important for roll-over relief or when considering the gift of the property; for the purposes of TCGA 1992, s. 165 (gifts of business assets) it is necessary to look over the period of ownership, necessitating good records over a long period of time.

Often the issue is not appreciated until late in the day, perhaps making it necessary to go back to the client to obtain further information and frequently requiring the re-preparation of certain basic information. It is therefore essential that the day count data is captured as part of the core financial records. For the reasons explained above this needs to be on a unit by unit basis but such data is often not captured. It can also be cumbersome to deal with deposits in order to get to a clear pattern of occupancy across the period concerned.

It is particularly important to understand the period concerned, and the position in respect of furnished holiday lettings and the first period of trading is often misunderstood. In such cases data will frequently have to be obtained on the day count test in respect of the period beyond 5 April of the year in which the accounts have been prepared. As considered further in **Chapters 2** and **7**, it is also necessary to consider whether the FHLs are part of a larger trading business or a standalone land and property business. In this respect the VAT position (see **Chapter 8**) is important and it is therefore essential that there is clarity of thinking on all these taxes.

The best way to deal with the issues in respect of qualifying criteria, i.e. as to whether a furnished holiday lettings activity is being carried on, is to ensure that there is a working paper on the accounts or tax file that shows the relevant tests on a unit by unit basis. This should be prepared each year so as to provide a permanent record for dealing with HMRC queries or to enable appropriate tax planning to be undertaken. Any private use of a property must also be fully considered so that the appropriate adjustments (as considered in **Chapter 1**) are made in the accounts.

4. Furnished holiday letting in the EEA

4.1 Introduction

The motivation for the government to introduce changes to the furnished holiday lettings regime was the concern over the historic restrictions of the rules to UK properties only. This was considered to be discriminatory under EU rules and so an extension of the special tax regime to the EEA was decided upon. In the course of discussions with HM Treasury and HMRC during the consultative process, it became clear that there was no detailed analysis of the implications, or assessment of the tax impact at stake for the UK exchequer. There is therefore very little to go on as to the likely impact of this change.

FA 2011 deems the extension of the rules to properties in the EEA to have always been in force. For income tax purposes it introduces new sections 328A (capital allowances) and 328B (pensions) into ITTOIA 2005 and a new section 127ZA (losses) into ITA 2007. For corporation tax purposes CTA 2009, s. 269A (capital allowances) and CTA 2010, s. 67A (losses) are the only new sections required. Consequential amendments are also made to CAA 2001, (s. 17A, 17B and 250A) and to TCGA 1992, s. 241A. Finally, the ability to allocate income unequally on a jointly owned property as between a married/civil partnership couple in ITA 2007, s. 836 is extended to include an EEA furnished holiday lettings business.

The result of this is that there are now four categories of property income business for UK tax purposes:

1. UK furnished holiday lettings business;
2. EEA furnished holiday lettings business;
3. ordinary UK property business; and
4. ordinary overseas property business.

Therefore, for UK tax purposes, commercial letting of furnished holiday accommodation in more than one EEA state (other than the UK) is to be combined into a single EEA furnished holiday lettings business. However, in most cases it is likely that clients will only have an EEA furnished holiday lettings business in a single non-UK EEA state.

These changes give rise to a number of issues in terms of dealing with more than one tax authority and practical reporting difficulties. For the other EEA states the reporting of income will invariably be on a calendar year basis. Depending on the numbers there may be practical difficulties in re-computing the figures and in matching the overseas tax paid against the income as reported for UK purposes.

4.2   What does EEA state mean?

The new legislation in ITTOIA 2005, s. 322 refers to "EEA states" and ITA 2007, s. 127ZA uses the definition of an "EEA furnished holiday lettings business" within the meaning of ITTOIA 2005, Pt. 3, chapter 6 and so is based upon a reference to EEA states.

Surprisingly, the income tax legislation does not contain a separate definition of "EEA" or of "EEA states", nor is there any existing definition of EEA within any other tax legislation. However, the Interpretation Act 1978 states:

"'EEA states', in relation to any time, means –

A state which at that time is a member State;" or

Any other state which at that time is a party to the EEA agreement."

The same Act also states that:

"'EEA agreement' means the agreement on the European Economic Area signed at Oporto on 2nd May 1992, together with a Protocol adjusting that Agreement signed at Brussels on 17th March 1993, as modified or supplemented from time to time".

So EEA means European Economic Area which is a combination of the EU and the European Free Trade Association (EFTA), in order to form the largest possible free trade area within Europe. However, since the EEA was formed a number of countries have left EFTA to become part of the EU.

There are currently 27 members of the EU namely:

Austria	Germany	Netherlands
Bulgaria	Greece	Poland
Belgium	Hungary	Portugal
Cyprus	Ireland	Romania
Czech Republic	Italy	Slovakia
Denmark	Latvia	Slovenia
Estonia	Lithuania	Spain
Finland	Luxembourg	Sweden
France	Malta	UK

Of the four members of EFTA only three are members of the EEA being Iceland, Norway and Liechtenstein.

Switzerland is a member of EFTA but is not an EEA state. This is important to appreciate as it is very common for UK residents to own ski chalets or other holiday accommodation in Switzerland. Such lettings can only generate furnished lettings income (as an ordinary overseas property business) and cannot qualify for the special FHL rules. However, alpine properties in the neighbouring countries would be taxed as furnished holiday lettings if they met the necessary criteria.

That deals with mainland Europe, subject to the proviso that there are various countries that are seeking to join the EU and therefore the EEA. At the moment talks are on-going with Albania, Bosnia-Herzegovina, Croatia, Iceland, Macedonia, Montenegro, Serbia and Turkey.

However, the position becomes more confusing when one looks at the various former overseas colonies of the European countries. The difficulty here is that these are very likely to be locations in which UK residents would undertake the letting of holiday accommodation. These are mainly islands around Europe and across the Atlantic, Indian Ocean and the Pacific. These locations are split into two categories being:

- outermost regions, and
- overseas countries and territories (OCTs).

Whilst there is plenty of scope for confusion, and matters are not entirely free from doubt, the position is that outermost regions are within the EU and therefore the EEA whereas OCTs are not within the EEA.

4.3 Outermost regions and OCTs

There are nine outermost regions as follows:

Outermost Regions	Location	Part of
Azores	Atlantic	Portugal
Canaries	Atlantic	Spain
Guadeloupe	Caribbean	France
French Guiana	South America	France
Madeira	Atlantic	Portugal
Martinique	Caribbean	France
Réunion	Indian Ocean	France
Saint Barthélemy	Caribbean	France
Saint Martin	Caribbean	France

It was unclear for some time whether Saint Barthélemy and Saint Martin were outermost region or OCTs and in October 2010 it was announced by the French government that Saint Barthélemy would become an OCT as of 1 January 2012. Conversely the current overseas department of Mayotte will become an outermost region in 2014. There has been no guidance from HMRC as to how such changes in status are to be dealt with for the purposes of the FHL rules.

The OCTs are potentially very confusing in terms of interpreting the meaning of EEA state. This is because it is easy to confuse them with parts of the EU as many of them are part of the Eurozone. In some cases they have the right to vote in EU elections and have residents who are EU citizens, as well as operating as if they are part of the EEA in terms of the freedom of movement of goods, services and individuals.

There are 22 OCTs as follows:

Name of territory	Country with historic connection
Anguilla	UK
Bermuda	UK
British Antarctic Territory	UK
British Indian Ocean Territory	UK
British Virgin Islands	UK
Cayman Islands	UK
Faulkton Islands	UK
Montserrat	UK
Pitcairn Islands	UK
Saint Helena, Ascension and Tristan da Cunha	UK
South Georgia and the South Sandwich Islands	UK
Turks and Caicos Islands	UK
Saint-Pierre	France
Miquelon	France
French Polynesia	France
Wallis and Futuna	France
French Southern and Antarctic Lands	France
Clipperton Island	France
Aruba	Netherlands
Curaçao	Netherlands
Sint Maarten	Netherlands
Greenland	Denmark

4.4 Other possible locations

There are then 11 further special cases which do not sit simply within either the outermost region or OCTs categories. These further locations are:

Åland Islands
Büsingen am Hochrhein
Campione d'Italia and Livigno
Ceuta and Melilla
The Channel Islands and the Isle of Man
Cyprus
Faroe Islands
Gibraltar
Heligoland
Mount Athos
Saimaa Canal and Malyj Vysotskij Island

The Channel Islands and the Isle of Man are not part of the EEA and therefore properties let in those locations cannot qualify as furnished holiday lettings.

The position of Cyprus is more complex for a number of reasons. One of them is the partition of the island into north and south Cyprus. Northern Cyprus is not part of the EEA and therefore properties let in that part of the island cannot qualify as furnished holiday lettings for the purposes of the special tax legislation. The status of the buffer zone between the two parts of the island is uncertain although it is unlikely that anyone will be letting property in that location. A further area of complication is that there are two UK sovereign bases on Cyprus (Akrotiri and Dhekelia) which appear to be *de facto* treated as part of the EU although their status is somewhat more uncertain than that.

The most tricky location seems to be Gibraltar. Citizens of Gibraltar vote in EU elections as part of the south west constituency of the UK and Gibraltar is a full member of the EU. It has its own government and is a separate jurisdiction to the UK. It is required to transpose EU directives through its own domestic legislation rather than being treated as part of the UK. However the UK government bodies do not regard it as an EEA state and it is not a party to the EEA agreement as required by the Interpretation Act 1978. It is therefore something of an oddity.

Part of the reason for the unique status of Gibraltar may be the historic antagonism between the UK and Spain over sovereignty – but relations are improving. Its tax status in the eyes of the UK authorities may change but in the meantime the different treatment of holiday letting in Gibraltar as opposed to other locations in the EU must be open to an accusation of discrimination. This is more pertinent given that Gibraltar is a holiday destination and there will be properties that will be prevented from obtaining the benefit of FHL status because of the restrictive EEA definition used.

For anyone looking to maintain a case that the definition of EEA state is discriminatory, reference to the ECJ case of *Prunus* would be appropriate. The decision was released by the ECJ on 5 May 2011. The case concerned the application of French tax law to the British Virgin Islands as an OCT. The ECJ held that the OCTs were outside of the EU for these purposes and therefore there was no discrimination as far as the French tax laws were concerned. However, the decision is quite limited in its scope and whilst this certainly helps in terms of assisting in the understanding of the relationship with the OCTs, it does not necessarily shed much light on some of the more complex special case scenarios.

A location either joining, or leaving, the EEA is a potential difficulty in terms of applying the EEA furnished holiday lettings business rules. This would not appear to benefit from the period of grace provisions and such changes will give rise to the commencement, or cessation, of a business.

Case: *Prunus (C-384/09, ECJ)*

4.5   Overseas ownership arrangements

In the UK it is most common for furnished holiday lettings to be undertaken by individuals either as sole traders or through partnerships. It is less common for companies to own holiday letting properties except in the case of very large operators. This pattern is not true of foreign jurisdictions. Indeed the pattern will vary considerably between territories with legal systems derived from the UK, those largely applying Roman law, and former communist block countries. Properties may therefore be owned outright, through trust or foundation structures or through some kind of corporate vehicle. Such structures may be opaque or transparent for UK tax purposes. It is therefore important to quiz the property owner carefully to ensure that the arrangements are fully understood before considering how the UK furnished holiday lettings rules apply. For instance in Bulgaria it has not been possible for non-residents to own land and so Bulgarian companies have been used as intermediate vehicles. In France, Spain and Portugal, company ownership has typically been adopted to avoid forced heirship rules.

It may be that a company has been used to acquire an overseas property as nominee; as long as proper trust documentation has been prepared, the beneficial ownership will still rest with the individual who will be taxable on it in his or her own capacity.

It is only necessary to consider the UK tax implications of the FHL rules for overseas companies where it is considered that the central management and control of the company is based in the UK. In this context it is also necessary to consider shadow directors.

4.6   Benefits in kind – living accommodation

The problem over the ownership of overseas properties by limited companies for local legal reasons was recognised by the government in FA 2008 which introduced ITEPA 2003, s. 100A and s. 100B. These provisions are designed to ensure that benefits in kind do not arise in certain circumstances. It was felt necessary to introduce this concession following the growth in the ownership of overseas properties in this way and the implications of the existing case law, specifically *Regina v Dimsey & Allan*. This exempting legislation is designed to apply to holiday homes generally whereas our subject is the narrower one of commercially let properties.

The HMRC Employment Income Manual does provide some further guidance on the calculation and benefits in kind – specifically at paragraphs 11421 to 11423. These paragraphs consider an example using similar facts but with a slightly different scenario in each case to demonstrate HMRC's view as to how benefits in kind should be assessed. In the context of considering commercially let FHL accommodation, the most appropriate example is in EIM 11422. This deals with establishing the meaning of "availability" as far as the benefits in kind income tax legislation is concerned. The paragraph states:

"A UK company purchases a flat in a French ski resort for £200,000. It is agreed that the market rental for the property would be £500 per week during the six month skiing season and £100 per week during the rest of the year. A husband and wife who are both directors of the company use the flat for holidays with their children for three weeks during the ski season and one week in the rest of the year. Their children are neither employees nor directors of the company. The company bought the property to let as a commercial letting business. They have employed professional agents to let the property and have managed to let the property for 12 weeks of the year in addition to the period it was used by the husband and wife directors.

In this case, we would accept that provided is equivalent to actual use.

If the cost of the accommodation exceeds £75,000, then the amount of the cash equivalent will be calculated in accordance with Section 106 ITEPA 2003 (see EIM 11472). As the annual value is based on the open market rental, under ESC A91 the Inland Revenue restricts the cash equivalent of the benefit to step 1 of Section 106. This would mean that the cash equivalent for the tax year would be £1,200 (£15,600 x 4/52). Under Section 108 ITEPA 2003 that will be split between the husband and wife in whatever way was just and reasonable, presumably half each in this case (see EIM 11472).

You may ask why the Section 105 ITEPA 2003 charge is not £1,600 (being three weeks at £500 in the skiing season and one week at £100 outside the season). The answer is that the wording written in Section 105(3) requires us to look at a proportion of the annual rent rather than the rent for the actual weeks it was used."

It should be appreciated, when advising on overseas properties, that it is far more likely that they will be owned through corporate structures and that benefit in kind issues will therefore arise than is the case with properties in the UK. It is important that such benefits in kind are not overlooked.

Case: *Regina v Dimsey & Allen* [1999] BTC 335.

4.7 Taxes in other EEA states

There are likely to be a considerable variety of taxes due on an overseas property within the EEA. These will probably include a tax on income generated from the letting of the property, as well as local property taxes (the equivalent of rates or council tax) and also wealth taxes or other levies on capital.

It is important to appreciate that the rental income and expenditure computation is likely to be calculated on a different basis as between the UK and the other EEA state(s). Relief for capital expenditure will probably be on a different basis and deductible reliefs may also be different – either more or less. For instance, it may well be appropriate to claim relief in the UK for travel costs in connection with visiting the property but these may well not be relievable in the other EEA state(s).

Further, the statement of FHL rental income and expenditure for UK purposes will have to be in sterling – either converted on an expense by expense basis or more likely using average rates for each month of the year. The impact of currency exchange differences means that the resulting profit or loss could be very different for UK tax purposes than that used in the EEA state concerned. This has implications for the treatment of any foreign tax suffered as to how it should be treated in the relevant UK tax return (see below).

The treatment of borrowing costs may also be a major difference between the assessable FHL income and that arising in the relevant EEA state(s). This could be because of restrictions on tax relief on interest costs in the EEA state(s) concerned but may also be because the funding is in a different currency.

The most significant difference in terms of offset of foreign tax suffered tends to apply on capital gains. In part this is because of the increased variety of taxation approaches but it is also because of the greater sums involved and the longer time scales to be considered. The latter point means that currency movements have more impact on the resulting UK tax position. Apart from differences in tax rates, there may also be indexation relief, tapering of gains over time, rebasing and owner occupation reliefs to consider. Whilst in some cases there may be considerable attraction to the availability of entrepreneurs' relief on the sale of a furnished holiday lettings property in an EEA state, it may be that the foreign tax suffered is considerably greater such that no benefit is obtained compared to an 18 or 28 per cent tax rate.

Finally, although unrelated to the UK tax position, it is also important for owners to consider the relevant local VAT treatment of holiday accommodation income in the EEA state(s) concerned.

4.8   Double tax agreements and double tax relief

As is to be expected in the EEA, double tax agreements are almost universally in place. The only exception is Liechtenstein. Further, the double tax agreements in each case are largely modern, expansive and based on the OECD model treaty. The only oddities are the absence of reference to the treatment of capital gains in the agreement with Cyprus and to the treatment of income from immoveable property in the agreement with Greece. However, given the difficulties in the UK of defining the boundary between rental income and trading that are thrown up by the commercial letting of holiday accommodation, it is important not just to assume that the income is derived from immoveable property rather than being business profits. Whilst "immoveable property" generally has a fairly wide meaning (to include income from agriculture and forestry) it must be construed in accordance with the law of the country concerned.

The letting of a single property in an overseas jurisdiction clearly comprises income from immoveable property – especially if an agent is involved, there are minimal additional services provided and there is no presence by the owner at the property during the course of the letting. However, at the other end of the spectrum it is possible to have an activity that could amount to a permanent establishment. This is likely to be very unusual and would probably have the following hallmarks:

- owner presence,
- a sizeable level of activity – such as a complex of villas,
- the provision of services that extend beyond the mere exploitation of land, and
- the existence of a business enterprise – such as the use of a company.

It is therefore imperative that local advice is taken in the EEA state concerned - but in general it is likely to be the case that the income is from immoveable property.

Relief for foreign tax paid is primarily by credit against UK tax in accordance with TIOPA 2010, Pt. 2. The main point to watch for here is that the foreign tax qualifies for relief in accordance with TIOPA 2010, s. 21 and more specifically in TIOPA 2010, s. 106 which requires the foreign tax on gains to be "of a similar character to capital gains tax".

Despite the aggregation of all commercial letting of furnished holiday accommodation within the EEA by an owner into a single EEA business, relief for credit of foreign tax paid is still restricted to the UK liability arising on a source by source basis. Where there is no tax liability (or only a minimal UK tax liability) then it may be better to elect against credit relief under TIOPA 2010, s. 27. The foreign tax would then be allowed as a deduction in the computation of the income or gain in accordance with TIOPA 2010, s. 112 and s. 113.

Electing against credit relief is likely to be beneficial where the FHL treatment in the UK entitles the owner to more deductions in the computation of taxable income than in the foreign jurisdiction. This could well be due to the capital allowances regime, especially in the first period of letting. It is usually most appropriate where there is a loss for UK tax purposes and the benefit is to use the foreign tax paid to increase the loss carried forward for UK income tax purposes.

4.9   Non-domiciliaries and the remittance basis

It does, of course, need to be borne in mind that where a non-UK domiciled individual is carrying on a furnished holiday lettings business in another EEA state(s) then the remittance basis may apply. There are three circumstances in which the remittance basis in ITA 2007, Pt. 14, chapter A1 could apply to income or gains from an EEA furnished holiday lettings business:

1. a short term UK resident (less than seven out of the last nine preceding years of assessment) has unremitted income or gains and claims the remittance basis without payment of the remittance basis charge (RBC);

2. a long term UK resident has unremitted income or gains and claims the remittance basis and pays the RBC; or
3. the UK resident has unremitted income or gains and the remittance basis applies automatically (ITA 2007 s. 809D) because the amount is below the *de minimis* limit (£2,000 for 2011/12).

All three scenarios are quite likely to be encountered by tax advisers in practice. Whilst it is unlikely that an EEA furnished holiday lettings business alone would cause an individual to pay the RBC, it is perfectly conceivable that a wealthy non-UK domiciled individual may have an EEA furnished holiday lettings business within his or her non-UK assets. It is very possible that a short term non-UK domiciled individual could have an EEA furnished holiday lettings business – especially if the individual is domiciled in an EEA state. Finally, whilst the *de minimis* limit is unlikely ever to apply to gains, income from an EEA furnished holiday lettings business for a year could be less than £2,000 if there is a high level of expenditure – such as in the start-up year.

Therefore, it is important that the domicile position of an individual operating an EEA furnished holiday lettings business is considered and advice given on the remittance basis at a very early stage. It is imperative that funds are not repatriated to the UK unwittingly from the business and therefore all trading income and expenses should be deposited in, or paid out of, an overseas bank account. A particular pitfall to watch out for is that the income from the EEA furnished holidays letting business is not used to pay for UK expenses in a way that the owner might consider to be a valid business expense but that HMRC would view as a remittance. Specifically, the cost of travelling to the property in the EEA state concerned should be paid for from UK source funds and not from the EEA furnished holiday lettings business bank account.

5.   Investing in furnished holiday lettings

5.1   Introduction

The specific tax issues to consider for those investing in furnished holiday lettings relate both to property income and to trading income. This is to be expected, given that FHLs sit across the divide between these two types of activity. Added to this, FHL property owners are a broad church, extending from those letting a single property attached to their home to operators of a large number of units. Whether the owner carries on other business activities such as a farm or an hotel is also relevant, and whilst VAT is probably one of the first issues to consider on a purchase of a property, the VAT issues are not specific to FHLs.

VAT matters are considered more specifically in **Chapter 8**. This chapter concentrates instead on the tax issues that directly relate to the acquisition of FHL properties. In that respect, the personal circumstances of the owners will be the main determinant of the ownership structure to be adopted and of the tax issues that apply.

This chapter examines the tax issues to take into account when determining how FHLs should be acquired and then considers some capital allowance issues peculiar to the nature of the activity.

5.2   Ownership structuring for a furnished holiday lettings business

There are many tax and financing issues to consider on the acquisition of a furnished holiday lettings business. Many of these are not peculiar to the activity concerned, but it is perhaps helpful here to consider some of the most commonly encountered issues.

5.2.1   Spouses and civil partners

As far as income tax is concerned, the most sensible ownership arrangement is for the property to be owned jointly. This is because (unlike the position with ordinary property businesses) ITA 2007, s. 837(3) provides an exception to the normal rule that income must be apportioned equally between a married or civil partnership couple; instead, it can be allocated in whatever proportion the two owners choose. In this respect it is treated the same as a husband and wife trading partnership. This is a very flexible arrangement but there are other issues to consider. In particular, VAT will be relevant if there is an existing business making taxable supplies. It is therefore common, where there is another business activity, to have separate ownership of the FHL business in order to try to disaggregate the activities for VAT purposes. This is often encountered with farms, bed and breakfasts and hotels. In these cases one activity may be carried on by one of the couple with another activity being carried on by the couple jointly.

Depending on the age of the couple, and their personal circumstances, it may also be relevant to consider inheritance tax matters. Specifically in the case of a second marriage, there may be complex will provisions to prevent the property from passing to the survivor on the first death. Such cases would need careful discussion with the parties concerned.

5.2.2 Working tax credits

The question here is whether the activity amounts to working hours for the purposes of working tax credits. It has been known for the Tax Credit Office to give different answers on this point which in turn goes back to the heart of the issue as to whether any profits of the FHLs activity amount to "earned income" or to "investment income".

As explained in **Chapter 8**, working tax credits are available to the self-employed but not to property businesses. Therefore, whilst there will be other implications such as the minimum wage to consider, it is unlikely that the Tax Credit Office would dispute the working hours point if a limited company were to be used as the owner.

The important point here is that the special FHL status applies only for income tax, corporation tax and capital gains tax and so does not apply for working tax credits purposes.

5.2.3 Trading activity

Consideration should be given to the question of whether or not the FHL business amounts to a trade. This is considered in detail in **Chapter 2**. If the activity does amount to a trade, this will have a number of implications, including a bearing on the overall structuring of the business, so this should be considered at a very early stage. In particular, owner's accommodation on site is likely to make a difference on this point.

5.2.4   Company ownership

Most FHLs are individually owned. Trustee ownership is possible, as are company structures. Owners of a large number of units are often companies, although in many cases these may be trading businesses in their own right. Some incorporated farms may have FHL income although care is required over the ownership arrangement here: it may be that the property is actually owned individually, in which case there would need to be appropriate tenancy agreements in place.

Ignoring very large complexes, the use of companies is likely to be driven by factors other than the nature of the property itself. These may be because the owners wish to involve a pension scheme (see **5.3** below) or wish to avoid having more income in their own names for personal income tax reasons. Company structuring can also be useful in terms of succession planning. However, there are downsides, including the lack of availability of main residence relief under TCGA 1992, s. 222 and an actual or potential benefit in kind under ITEPA 2003, s. 102. The issues over main residence relief and benefits in kind are particularly likely to arise in respect of FHL businesses where owners' accommodation is included.

In most cases there will be no additional tax reliefs available to a company that would not be available to an individual or a trustee. This is not true, though, if goodwill has been acquired that would be eligible for amortisation under CTA 2009, Pt. 8. However, a warning here is that such goodwill is likely to be trade-related as far as the property is concerned and so HMRC will be likely to argue that SDLT is still due on the acquisition price to the extent that it relates to trade-related goodwill. HMRC will challenge any high value given to goodwill for amortisation under the intangible asset regime. Fundamentally, this is an issue of valuation, but there is dispute over the basis on which the valuation should be arrived at. Where this is significant, a specialist valuer should be involved.

5.2.5   Business property relief

The availability of business property relief should be considered in the context of IHTA 1994, s. 105(3) (see, also, **Chapter 8**). In particular, attention must be paid to the overall business being carried on and to the question of whether it is wholly or mainly one of holding investments. This is most likely to be a consideration where other activities are carried on by the owners. It may be appropriate to try to separate the FHL business in some way or alternatively to argue for it to be part of a larger business activity in accordance with *Farmer* and *Balfour* cases.

5.2.6   Rollover relief

Where this has been claimed under TCGA 1992, s. 152, the ownership will need to follow that of the person making the gain. In the past, a planning technique has been to shelter capital gains of individuals making business sales who then reinvest into FHLs, take them into use and carry on the activity for a period of time; they may subsequently cease the furnished holiday lettings activity and use the property within an ordinary property business. Where such an approach has been followed, the owner must be the one making the gain which may be only one half of a married couple, though it is perfectly possible for the property to be transferred into joint ownership at a later date without the gain crystallising.

Another scenario where rollover relief is a driving force is where, for instance, a farmer sells fields which would not qualify for entrepreneurs' relief and then reinvests the money into the conversion of redundant farm buildings into self-catering accommodation. This is a common planning scenario and would again determine the ownership structure.

It is important to remember that for rollover relief to apply it is a condition that the asset must be taken into use on acquisition. This condition can still be met where there are building works prior to bringing the property into use, but in such a case careful planning is required in order to ensure that the necessary conditions are met.

5.2.7   New build properties

The age and nature of the property must be considered, in addition to the question of whether it is currently in use as a furnished holiday letting. As well as tax issues there may be planning restrictions to consider. However, in cases of new build properties, the main tax issue to consider will be VAT as the supply of new build holiday accommodation is taxable and so the purchaser will need to consider how best to recover the VAT concerned. For an existing business, it may be that the transfer is a TOGC, which will again mean that there are VAT issues to address. These issues are considered further in **Chapter 8**.

The above paragraphs cover a number of the most commonly encountered issues. The main thing, though, is to consider matters fully considered on acquisition. Too often, mistakes are made in the initial structuring of an FHL business, resulting in an unfortunate increase in the tax liability for the owner(s) concerned.

Cases: *Farmer & Anor (Exors of Frederick Farmer dec'd) v IRC* (1999) Sp C 216; *HMRC v A M Brander as Exec of the Will of the late fourth Earl of Balfour* [2010] UKUT 300 (TCC)

5.3   Use of pension schemes

The use of a pension scheme in the ownership of an FHL property can be very tax efficient. Operating FHL accommodation owned by a pension fund will enable the rent paid for the use of the property to be tax deductible for income or corporation tax purposes in the FHL business. There will be no tax to pay by the pension scheme on any rent received or capital growth and this will be able to accumulate in the fund tax-free.

There is a prohibition on the use of pension schemes to invest in residential property. However, for these purposes FHL properties may be considered to be commercial rather than residential. The commercial status of property is not free from doubt and in reality it is likely to be the attitude of the individual Self Invested Personal Pension (SIPP) or Small Self Administered Scheme (SSAS) provider that matters. Many providers will simply not be interested in trying to deal with the purchase of holiday accommodation into a SIPP or a SSAS but there are some that will be prepared to handle the purchase of such an asset.

The position becomes more straightforward the more clearly commercial the property concerned is. For instance, if there is an occupancy restriction over the property then it is clearly not residential, or if the property is being purchased as part of an hotel and self-catering complex then again matters are more straightforward. Certainly if there is owner's accommodation as part of any FHL complex then this will not be eligible for ownership within a SIPP or a SSAS.

The use of a SIPP or a SSAS does introduce complexity into the ownership structure. Therefore, it would be necessary to assess whether such complications in the ownership structure are worthwhile. It will also be important to think about the treatment of capital allowances on any integral features in the property as these will not be a benefit to the SIPP or the SSAS. It will be important to consider the lease arrangements in this respect. Where a property is owned by a pension scheme then an arm's length commercial lease will be required.

Some SIPP and SSAS providers will also consider ownership of overseas property and so it is possible that a pension scheme could be used to purchase FHL property in the EEA outside of the UK. However, this is very unlikely to permit use by the owner when the property is not let.

A pension scheme could be used in other ways rather than just for the purchase of the property. A loan back arrangement would be possible although this would necessitate the use of a company, which may be undesirable for other reasons. The other downside of a loan back would be the relatively short period of time over which capital repayments will be required which may be unattractive from a cash flow point of view. However, there are certainly circumstances whereby a SSAS arrangement could be attractive, particularly if there are existing pension funds and a company owner is considered to be an appropriate form of structuring. Loans could be taken from the pension scheme to help fund fixtures and fittings and such an approach could work well for all concerned.

A final point is that whilst such structuring may be tax efficient, it may not be appropriate from a retirement income perspective. In particular, it is important to remember that property is an illiquid asset class.

5.4   Tax relief on improvement and acquisition expenditure

In accordance with CAA 2001, s. 15, capital allowances are available on an ordinary UK property business, a UK furnished holiday lettings business, an ordinary overseas property business and an EEA furnished holiday lettings business. The relevant rules in respect of entitlement to capital allowances for UK furnished holiday lettings businesses and for EEA furnished holiday lettings businesses are contained in CAA 2001, s. 17 and 17B. These adopt the qualifying criteria for the commercial letting of FHL in ITTOIA 2005 and CTA 2009. However, since all four types of property business qualify for capital allowances the really crucial factor is that CAA 2001, s. 35 does not prohibit the claiming of capital allowances in a dwelling-house where an FHL activity is carried on.

There was a further change introduced by FA 2011 in respect of claims for capital allowances in respect of property businesses. This change acknowledged that some owners may carry on more than one type of property business and that plant and machinery may be taken from one business to another. Therefore, CAA 2001, s. 13B provides that where a person carrying on any of the four types of property business uses plant and machinery in rotation between more than one business, that person is treated as transferring the item from one business to the other at the lower of original cost or market value.

Entitlement to capital allowances follows all the normal rules including the annual investment allowance, first-year allowance, normal writing-down allowances, short and long life asset rules and those for integral features. The ability to claim capital allowances is seen as one of the key attractions of the FHL regime and the potential loss of these allowances was a concern when the abolition of the regime was proposed. This is because the annual investment allowance provides a rapid form of tax relief whereas the alternative of wear and tear allowance or renewals basis would not provide the same incentive for upgrading furniture and furnishings. There are particular issues in respect of dwellings, considered at **5.5** below.

In the main, capital allowances are claimed on two different types of assets within a property used in a furnished holiday lettings business. The claim in respect of furniture and furnishings is both fairly obvious and has been historically very attractive because of first-year allowances, the annual investment allowance and writing-down allowances. The other category, though, is integral features and this is not always picked up or even appreciated. Indeed it is necessary to consider first the distinction between revenue and capital expenditure on properties used in FHL businesses.

As with similar trading activities involving the use of properties, the two cases of *Law Shipping Company Limited v CIR* and *Odeon*

Associated Theatres Limited v Jones are extremely relevant. The key distinction was whether the asset was able to be used for the purposes of the activity at the time of acquisition. In the case of Odeon Cinemas, the company acquired "flea pit" cinemas that had been run down because of war-time restrictions and that needed substantial refurbishment. However, they were in use as cinemas when acquired and so the substantial expenditure was revenue in nature as the asset was always useable – just not very nice. In the case of properties used as holiday accommodation, if a property is acquired that is used in an existing FHL business then it can be substantially refurbished and the expenditure treated as revenue. This is in the case where expenditure is being incurred on the fabric of the building such as replacing windows, doors, plasterwork, roofs etc.

The result was that it was possible to have very large loss claims as a combination of annual investment allowance on a substantial replacement of largely worthless furniture and furnishings and a very large revenue claim in respect of improvements to the fabric of the building. This approach has been used by certain people to buy a run-down FHL cottage, trade it for a season, substantially refurnish it, make a large income tax loss relief claim and then after trading it for a further season or two sell the property at a substantial profit on which capital gains tax was paid at only 10 per cent. There was therefore a tax arbitrage as the expenditure was relieved for tax at 40 per cent and the gain only taxed at 10 per cent. This was one of the things that the government found unacceptable about relieving losses against other income.

However, it is important to consider the nature of the capital expenditure and whether or not it is treated through the capital allowances regime. A claim for capital allowances is possible in respect of integral features, and the replacement of integral features should therefore be dealt with through the capital allowances regime. There is an argument that furniture and furnishings can be dealt with through the capital allowances regime with the other items being dealt with on a renewals basis although this is debatable and is considered further below. Also, where a substantial annual investment allowance was available then the difference in the two approaches was minimal but with a lower annual investment allowance the position changes and the renewals basis becomes more attractive. The position on integral features and the renewals basis are considered further below.

Cases: *Law Shipping Company Limited v CIR* (1923) 12 TC 621; *Odeon Associated Theatres Limited v Jones* (1971) 48 TC 257

5.5   Dwelling-houses

5.5.1   *Background and HMRC guidance*

Capital allowances are available to property businesses under CAA 2001, s. 17 but for ordinary property businesses are restricted from applying to expenditure "in a dwelling-house" by CAA 2001, s. 35. No such restriction applies to FHLs that meet the qualifying criteria. However, if the qualifying criteria are not met, then the restriction would apply, so the meaning of dwelling-house is potentially of very great significance if a property ceases to qualify for any reason.

It should be noted that section 35 refers to "dwelling-house", and not "dwelling" which is used in other parts of the Act. There is a definition of "dwelling-house" in CAA 2001, s. 531(1) which applies for the purposes of Part 10 (i.e. assured tenancy allowances rather than plant and machinery allowances), and states that it is to have "the same meaning as in the *Rent Act* 1977". However, the *Rent Act* 1977 does not have a defined term of "dwelling-house".

There have been concerns expressed by HMRC over entitlement to capital allowances in respect of residential accommodation so it is worth considering the current restriction further. Most recently, this concern has been over the treatment of student accommodation. R & C Brief 45/10 revised HMRC's interpretation of dwelling-house. This states that the definition in s. 531(1) is only to be taken to apply for the purposes of Part 10 of the Act and the term in s. 35 is to "take its ordinary everyday meaning". The HMRC view is that the reference to the *Rent Act* 1977 is to be read together with the *Housing Act* 1980.

The change of view arose as a result of HMRC's consideration of the implications of a case concerning the *Housing Act* 1988 (*Uratemp Ventures Ltd. v Collins*) which found that an hotel room could be a "dwelling-house", despite the absence of cooking facilities. The revised HMRC interpretation is based on the case of *Gravesham*

Borough Council v Secretary of State for the Environment. The Brief explains that:

> "against the background of the *Housing Act*, it was pointed out that the purpose of that Act was to give a measure of security to those who make their homes in rented accommodation, at the lower end of the housing market. And, in that particular context, a hotel room containing a shower and basin but no cooking facilities was found to constitute a separate dwelling. In *Gravesham* it was held that the distinctive feature of a dwelling house for the purposes of the *Town and Country Planning General Development Order*, since replaced by the *Use Classes Order*, was its ability to afford to those who use it the facilities required for day-to-day private domestic existence."

During the course of the consultation discussions with HMRC on the proposed changes to the FHL regime it became clear that there was quite a lot of head-scratching going on by HMRC, more generally over dwellings. There have also been suggestions by HMRC of unacceptable abuse of the capital allowances code in an attempt to secure allowances on what, in HMRC's view, were meant to be dwelling-houses. A particular concern is student accommodation and the HMRC view in R&C Brief 45/10 is that each flat in multiple occupation comprises a dwelling-house, given that the individual study bedrooms alone would not afford the occupants "the facilities required for day-to-day private domestic existence". In other words, the communal kitchen and lounge are also part of the dwelling-house. The common parts of the building block (such as the common entrance lobby, stairs or lifts) are not, however, part of a "dwelling-house".

The *Gravesham* case concerned the interpretation of "dwelling-house" for the *Town & Country Planning General Development Order* 1977 (since updated in 1995 to SI 1995/418). That Order contains the following interpretations:

- " 'dwelling-house' does not include a building containing one or more flats, or a flat contained within such a building;" and
- " 'flat' means a separate and self-contained set of premises constructed or adapted for use for the purpose of a dwelling and forming part of a building from some other part of which it is divided horizontally."

In *Gravesham* it was determined that

> "The Secretary of State could find that a building built under a permission for a weekend and holiday chalet, but to be used only in summer, was a dwelling-house. The distinctive characteristic of a dwelling-house is its ability to afford to those who use it the facilities required for day-to-day private domestic existence."

However, R&C Brief 45/10 mentions the *Use Classes Order* (SI 2010/653) but does seem to stretch this by extending dwelling-house to include lockable cluster flats of up to six flats with individual bedrooms and shared kitchen facilities, or to properties occupied by students where that property is not their main residence.

The issue for furnished holiday lettings is over the extent of the term "dwelling-house". Clearly, communal swimming pools and play equipment at a complex will always qualify for capital allowances as they are not part of the dwelling-house, and this interpretation is consistent with the view on the student accommodation. However, what proximity to a dwelling is permissible for such expenditure still to qualify?

Following R&C Brief 45/10 the guidance in the HMRC Capital Allowances Manual at 11520 states:

> "A person's second or holiday home or accommodation used for holiday letting is a dwelling-house. A block of flats is not a dwelling-house although the individual flats within the block may be. A hospital, a prison, a nursing home or hotel (run as a trade and offering services whether by the owner-occupier or by a tenant) are not dwelling houses."

The text in the HMRC Manual does now state that holiday accommodation used for letting is a dwelling-house. This is in direct contrast to the previous guidance which stated that it was not.

5.5.2   Other sources of guidance

"Dwelling" is referred to in other parts of the tax legislation, and there is a definition at CAA 2001, s. 393A for Flat Conversion Allowances. The term is also used in connection with determining taxable property for the pension legislation (FA 2004, Sch. 29A, para. 7–10).

In the VAT legislation at VATA 1994, Sch. 8, Grp 5, Note 2, a building must satisfy the following conditions if it is to be a dwelling:

- it is self-contained living accommodation;
- there is no provision for direct internal access from the dwelling to any other dwelling or part of a dwelling;
- separate use, or disposal, of the dwelling is not prohibited by the term of any covenant, statutory planning consent or similar provision; and
- statutory planning consent has been granted in respect of the dwelling and its construction, or conversion has been carried out in accordance with that consent.

Some assistance on the extent of the term dwelling-house may be provided by the stamp duty land tax legislation. The meaning of dwelling for SDLT is set out in FA 2003, Sch. 6A, para. 7 and is stated to include land occupied and enjoyed with the dwelling as its garden or grounds. This definition is clearly derived from that used for main residence relief for CGT purposes as it includes a "permitted area" of half a hectare or such larger area as is required for the reasonable enjoyment of the property. A similar definition is included in FA 2003, Sch. 9, para. 7(6) with reference to relief from SDLT for right to buy, shared ownership and certain related transactions, and in FA 2011, Sch. 22, para. 7 in respect of transfers of multiple dwellings. However, residential rates of SDLT only apply if the relevant land consists entirely of residential property, and the meaning of residential property in FA 2003, s. 116 includes a building used or suitable for use as a dwelling, or one that is in the process of being constructed or adapted for such use.

HMRC's current guidance on the extent of grounds to be treated as part of a residential property indicates that the CGT interpretation for main residence relief is to be used. The definition of dwelling-house was considered in *Batey v Wakefield* and so supports the HMRC view. Thus, where there is land around a dwelling in excess of what would be regarded as normal for TCGA 1992, s. 222, it would appear as though HMRC would interpret the whole property as non-residential for SDLT. However, remember that CAA 2001, s. 35 refers to "in a dwelling-house".

When considering the scope of the restriction in the term dwelling-house, it is also worth considering the terms "accommodation used for holiday letting" (the term used in the HMRC Capital Allowances Manual at 11520 prior to 22 October 2010), and "hotel". The nearest definition to "accommodation used for holiday letting" appears to be the definition of "holiday accommodation" for VAT where VATA 1994, Sch. 9, Grp. 1, Item 1(e) and Note 13 refers to:

> "any accommodation in a building, hut (including a beach hut or chalet), caravan, houseboat or tent which is advertised or held out as holiday accommodation or suitable for holiday use, but excludes any accommodation within paragraph (d)".

Paragraph 1(d) covers a hotel, inn, boarding house or similar establishment of sleeping accommodation or of accommodation in rooms which are provided in conjunction with sleeping accommodation or for the purpose of catering. "Similar establishment" is further clarified in Note 9 as including premises in which there is provided furnished sleeping accommodation, whether with or without the provision of board or facilities for the preparation of food, which are used by, or held out as being suitable for use by, visitors or travellers. The *Hotel Proprietors Act* 1956 defines an hotel as: "an establishment held out by the proprietor as offering food, drink and, if so required, sleeping accommodation, without special contract, to any traveller presenting himself who appears able and willing to pay a reasonable sum for the services and facilities provided and who is in a fit state to be received".

There is currently a lack of clarity over the tax definitions of "dwelling-house" and "accommodation for holiday letting". There is also scope for that confusion to spread for property tax purposes to the interpretation of "dwelling" and "hotel". It would not be surprising if there were a future attempt to restrict entitlement to capital allowances on such properties (a continuation of the policy of withdrawing industrial building allowances). Therefore, the issue of definition of dwelling and dwelling-house is of more than academic interest.

Cases: *Batey (Inspector of Taxes) v Wakefield* [1982] 1 All ER 61; *Gravesham Borough Council v Secretary of State for the Environment* (1982) 47 P&CR 142; *Uratemp Ventures Limited v* Collins (Ap) [2001] UKHL 43

5.6   Using the renewals basis

Furnished holiday lettings owners do not have to claim capital allowances but may instead opt for the renewals basis. Under this approach no capital allowances are claimed on the cost of an original item, or all the original items within one class, but the cost of replacement of that item, or those items, is a deductible expense under ITTOIA 2005, s. 68 or CTA 2009, s. 68. These both allow a deduction in calculating trading profits for expenditure on replacing or altering any implement, utensil or article used for the purposes of the trade. The Oxford English Dictionary defines "implement" as equipment and articles of furniture, "utensil" as an implement or vessel especially for domestic use and "article" as an item or commodity. These are primarily intended to be small items and the section is entitled "Replacement and alteration of trade tools". In addition, CAA 2001, s. 33B limits its use in circumstances where capital allowances could be claimed on an integral feature.

The disadvantage of the renewals basis is that relief is only available to the extent that like is replaced with like, any improvement element being disregarded, and no relief is available for additions to the class concerned, as opposed to replacements. However, it is attractive where the original cost of the capital items is low so that a full write-off of the expenditure on replacements is achieved in the year of acquisition. If the annual investment allowance is available on capital expenditure then there is little to be gained by the renewals basis, nor if a generous writing-down allowance applies. However, if the annual investment allowance is being used elsewhere then the renewals basis becomes more appropriate. This could be the case if the owner also operates a bed and breakfast or farming business.

The renewals basis ceased to be commonly used in the 1970s when first-year allowances became very generous. As a result there was little incentive to use the renewals basis so ESC B1 was introduced. This provides that:

> "Taxpayers who change from the "renewals" to the capital allowances basis are, however, permitted to claim such allowances as if the expenditure did so qualify provided that where they use more than one item of a class of machinery or

plant they change from the "renewals" basis to the capital allowances basis for all the items in that class."

There is no statutory procedure for transferring from claiming capital allowances to a renewals basis. It would seem that the change would have to involve bringing into account the market value disposal consideration for the items on which the renewals basis was being claimed. It is therefore unlikely to be worthwhile for an FHL business with a significant value of furniture and furnishings to move from capital allowances to renewals unless a significant replacement programme is intended and no annual investment allowance will be available.

Where there are furnished lettings that do not meet the qualifying criteria, capital allowances are not available in dwelling-houses (CAA 2001, s. 35). However, it is possible to elect under ITTOIA 2005, s. 308A or CTA 2009, s. 248A for a 10 per cent wear and tear allowance as an alternative to using the renewals basis. This is a statutory basis for what was ESC B47. A furnished property is one that is capable of normal occupation without the tenant having to provide their own beds, chairs, tables, sofa, cooker etc.

The wear and tear allowance is calculated by taking 10 per cent of the net rent received for the furnished residential accommodation. The "net rent" is calculated as gross rents less a deduction for charges and services that would normally be borne by a tenant but are, in fact, borne by the landlord (for example, council tax, water rates etc.). HMRC's view is that utilities should also be deducted, so in the case of holiday accommodation where the landlord is paying gas and electricity, these should be deducted in arriving at the "net rent". The wear and tear allowance is given to cover the cost of items that a tenant would normally provide in unfurnished accommodation; such as beds, televisions, cookers, fridges and freezers, carpets, curtains, linen, crockery or cutlery.

The HMRC Property Income Manual at 3200 states that "in addition to the 10% allowance, a taxpayer can also deduct the net cost of renewing or repairing fixtures that are an integral part of the buildings." This is because such expenditure is considered to be revenue expenditure on repairs. However, as mentioned above, this option may well not be available for FHLs because of CAA 2001, s. 33B. This point is considered further below.

Moving from being a qualifying FHL property to a non-qualifying property creates a computational complication that HMRC have been keen to avoid historically because of the assessment difficulties. The period of grace election is one of the measures designed to overcome this concern, so relatively few FHL properties should be forced to change from capital allowances to the wear and tear basis. Therefore the most common circumstance in which the wear and tear allowance may be encountered in respect of holiday lettings is where a property is only let on a seasonal basis for a few weeks each year.

5.7 Integral features and other fixtures

As explained above, it is relatively easy to identify capital allowances on furniture and furnishings but given the nature of the properties concerned there will be a substantial entitlement to capital allowances on fixtures in general and on integral features (as set out in CAA 2001, s. 33A) in particular. What qualifies as an integral feature is set out in subsection 5 of that section and broadly consists of electrical systems, cold water systems, heating and air conditioning, lifts and external solar shading subject to the usual proviso that if it is part of the main structure of the building (such as forming a wall or a floor) then it will not qualify. Fixtures that are not integral features include baths, showers, sinks, toilets, swimming pools and a variety of other assets.

The main differences in practice between integral features and other fixtures are twofold. On a positive note, integral features qualify as plant and machinery in their own right and the many case law difficulties about what constitutes plant simply disappear. On the other hand, integral features attract writing-down allowances at the lower rate only (as so-called "special rate expenditure"), whereas other fixtures are merged into the main pool and attract the standard rate of writing-down allowance. The annual investment allowance can, however, be claimed for both categories of expenditure.

There is a third difference in the treatment of integral features, though this arises less frequently in practice. This is a special rule that can apply when integral features are replaced (CAA 2001, s. 33B). Broadly this provides that if the expenditure on an integral feature amounts to more than 50 per cent of the cost of replacing that integral feature at the time the work is undertaken, then no revenue deduction is available for the work on that integral feature and it must be capitalised. This is a statutory limitation on the scope for using the renewals basis or claiming a revenue deduction for such expenditure.

It is fair to say that the rules on integral features and on fixtures in general are not well understood, especially in relation to the provision of furnished holiday lettings. As a rule, fixtures could comprise between 10 and 30 per cent of a property value, although perhaps a more likely range is 15 to 25 per cent. The bottom end of any such range will be basic properties with minimal equipment included in them. Higher percentages will apply to luxury, high specification properties which include air conditioning and a swimming pool. It is also important to remember that the entitlement to capital allowances on integral features applies equally to both UK and EEA furnished holiday lettings businesses.

To make a claim for allowances on a newly acquired property, it is necessary to prepare a reasonable apportionment of the purchase price in accordance with CAA 2001, s. 562. A specialist surveyor should be engaged to undertake this work, though many owners are reluctant to go to such expense. It is likely that such a claim would create a large loss, and where this can be used a substantial tax benefit will result. Alternatively, where the owner does not wish to go to the expense of engaging a specialist surveyor, it may be possible to make a relatively low claim based upon the knowledge and information readily available on the property. For instance, for a newly purchased property it may be relatively easy to justify a figure of 10 per cent of the acquisition price, though this will depend on various factors, including in particular the history of any claims made by previous owners and the question of whether any claim has been made since the integral features rules were introduced in 2008.

There is a surprising level of reluctance amongst owners to make such capital allowance claims on fixtures but it is important that professional advisers bring the claim to the attention of their clients in order to avoid a professional indemnity risk. There is a valid concern that while for certain clients a claim for allowances might generate an income tax rebate, that will only be a cash flow advantage because of a balancing charge arising on the sale of the property. This could be avoided if an election is entered into under CAA 2001, s. 198 but that will depend upon the bargaining position of the vendor on the sale of the property. Further CAA 2001, s. 13B is also relevant in this respect. Taking the property from being used within an FHL business to an ordinary property business would be a cessation for capital allowances purposes but would not open up the possibility of a s. 198 election. As a result it would crystallise a balancing charge. In this context, it should be noted that taking a property from being used within an FHL business to being on a long let is a common occurrence.

Example – acquisition of new property

Katie buys a new villa in Paphos in Cyprus for €300,000, which will be let commercially as holiday accommodation. It is a very high specification property and all year round occupancy is forecast. Katie does not own any other properties or have any other business interests. She has salaried employment in the UK. The property purchase is part funded with a €200,000 mortgage.

The property has its own swimming pool, air conditioning, solar panels and water recycling technology. A specialist firm of surveyors establishes that 30 per cent of the property value represents plant and machinery. In addition, Katie spends €20,000 furnishing the property.

For UK tax purposes a substantial capital allowance claim is possible. This will be at a mixture of rates of writing-down allowance and the annual investment allowance will also be due. It will generate a substantial loss for UK tax purposes. This loss and the future allowances can only be used against the profits from an EEA furnished holiday lettings property business (in this case only the Paphos property). Depending upon Katie's other income and foreign taxes suffered, it may in fact be better to disclaim some capital allowance now so that the benefit is received annually for many years into the future rather than have no income from the property at all in the early years due to losses and then higher profits subsequently.

Tax planning and considerations in respect of foreign tax suffered are set out in **Chapter 4**.

Example – refurbishment of a property

Sue buys a cottage used for furnished holiday letting in Bridport in Dorset for £250,000. The cottage has always qualified as a furnished holiday lettings but is tired and run down.

The seller had not made any claim previously for integral features. As a result, there is no dispute with the seller as to the figure to be placed on this plant and machinery on acquisition. A figure of £5,000 is placed on the furniture and furnishings. Sue discusses the proportion of the property qualifying as integral features with her professional advisers and makes a claim in respect of 10 per cent of the property.

During the first close season, Sue spends £93,000 completely renovating the property. It is necessary to consider how this should be allocated between revenue expenditure, energy saving plant and machinery, integral features and general pool plant and machinery.

The money spent on refurbishing the kitchen and bathroom and putting in a new en-suite relates to integral features. The replacement of the roof, repairs to windows, doors and flooring and redecoration are all revenue expenditure. The new boiler qualifies for energy saving plant treatment and the new furniture is put into the general pool (arguably renewals treatment would be better on the furniture).

The position is as follows:

	£
General pool – Furniture, carpets, sanitaryware etc.	35,000
Integral features – water, electrics etc.	20,000
Revenue – Refurbishment of property	34,000
Energy saving – New boiler etc.	4,000
	93,000

Note that revenue expenditure treatment through the renewals basis is not available on the kitchen, bathroom and en-suite expenditure qualifying as plant and machinery because of CAA 2001, s. 33B.

Integral features are a complex area and require more thought and consideration than is often given to them in practice.

5.8   Stamp duty land tax

A liability to SDLT will be expected to arise on the acquisition of an FHL business or an additional FHL property. Whilst there are no special rules in the SDLT legislation relating to furnished holiday lettings, it is worth commenting on some of the issues that typically arise, in particular those which sit on the boundary between residential and non-residential property.

The term "residential property" is defined in FA 2003, s. 116 as "a building that is used or suitable for use as a dwelling, or is in the process of being constructed or adapted for such use" and the legislation goes on to say that garden or grounds are included within this. "Non-residential property" is simply defined as that which is not residential property. An hotel, inn or similar establishment is excluded from the definition of residential property by FA 2003, s. 116 (3)(f).

A further point is that s. 116(7) provides that:

> "where six or more separate dwellings are the subject of a single transaction involved in the transfer of a major interest in, or the grant of release over, them, then, for the purposes of this Part as it applies in relation to that transaction, those dwellings are treated as not being residential property."

The issue of the meaning of dwelling as far as FHLs are concerned is considered at **5.5** above.

Clearly the treatment of residential against non-residential is relevant in connection with the acquisition of FHL complexes where a number of letting units are concerned. In this context, it is also relevant to consider a change introduced by FA 2011 for SDLT purposes (see FA 2003, Sch. 6B) entitled "Transfers involving multiply dwellings". This applies in the case of the acquisition of more than one dwelling (or at least one dwelling and other property). The effect is that SDLT is to be calculated by reference to the consideration per dwelling rather than the total consideration applying. The benefit of this is that, potentially, a large amount of the SDLT is payable at only 1 per cent on such an acquisition as opposed to being at the 3, 4 or even 5 per cent rates.

A further issue to consider on acquisition of an existing business which is VAT registered is whether the TOGC provisions apply. This is relevant for SDLT purposes as SDLT is due on the VAT-inclusive consideration. If the TOGC provisions apply, there is therefore an absolute saving in SDLT, as opposed to only the cash flow saving for VAT purposes.

Another area where SDLT could be relevant is in connection with partnerships and the special rules that apply on a change in the constitution of a partnership under FA 2003, Sch. 15. This is a very complex area but was simplified by FA 2006 such that the more restrictive rules only apply for a "property-investment partnership" within the meaning of FA 2003, Sch. 15 para. 14(8). This is defined as a partnership "whose sole or main activity is investing or dealing in chargeable interests". Again, this highlights the boundary between investment and other activities and the nature of what is being carried on. The issue of SDLT and partnerships is in any case complex and does need careful consideration where there are changes, particularly on the addition or removal of property. In the context of FHLs, the issue is most likely to arise in connection with farming partnerships that also have FHL activities – probably as part of a main trade. Where there is an attempt to separate out such activities, or to bring them together, for other tax reasons such as inheritance tax or VAT, the SDLT rules on partnerships also need to be given due consideration.

6. Sale of a property

6.1 Introduction

Minimising capital gains tax on the sale of a furnished holiday lettings business is one of the most common areas where specialist tax advice is required. The ability to obtain a 10 per cent tax rate on sale is a major attraction as is also achieving main residence relief through owner occupation or otherwise rolling over a gain into another business. These issues are all covered in this chapter.

However, in addition to capital gains tax it is also important to consider other tax issues on sale – especially income tax in connection with the disposals of plant and machinery (including fixtures). It is therefore important to consider the capital allowances position fully and this may be a source of some negotiation with a potential purchaser.

Finally, there are VAT issues to consider on a sale and the TOGC provisions may well apply. It is therefore important that VAT is considered and VAT matters, as more generally addressed in **Chapter 8**.

6.2 Availability of entrepreneurs' relief

For many owners, one of the main attractions of the special FHL rules is entitlement to entrepreneurs' relief and a 10 per cent capital gains tax rate on the sale of a property. Entrepreneurs' relief is available (subject to certain conditions) to an FHL business conducted by a sole trader, a partnership or a company. However, entrepreneurs' relief is not available to an FHL business operated by trustees. A trust may own the properties but the activity would have to be undertaken by a beneficiary with an interest in possession in order to get the relief.

Entrepreneurs' relief is available on furnished holiday lettings open in the UK or the EEA by virtue of TCGA 1992, s. 169S(1) (per s. 241(3A) and s. 241A(5)). The only other point to note in this context is that the definition of business assets in s. 169L(4)(b) excludes "assets ... which are held as investments". This is a difficult exclusion to interpret and "investments" is not a defined term. Given that FHLs are specifically legislated to qualify for entrepreneurs' relief, it is difficult to see that this restriction applies to them in any way. However, this point is worth reflecting on when trying to interpret the relevant case law on the boundary between investment activities and the carrying on of a trade (see **Chapters 2 and 7**).

A common query raised on the disposal of an FHL property is where the property concerned is sold after the furnished holiday lettings business has ceased. However, as long as the sale is within three years of the date of cessation of the FHL business, the disposal will continue to qualify for entrepreneurs' relief in accordance with TCGA 1992, s. 169I(4). There is no restriction on the use to which the property can be put during the period from the cessation of the FHL business up to the date of sale. However it is a strict three year statutory time limit and the HMRC Capital Gains Manual at 64045 makes clear that HMRC have no discretion to extend that time limit.

The personal company definition for the purposes of entrepreneurs' relief is contained in TCGA 1992, s. 169S(3). This is extended to cover FHLs by virtue of s. 169S(5) which imports the legislation used for business asset hold-over relief and in particular s. 165A(14). However, the legislation that is currently drafted only cross refers to TCGA 1992, s. 241(3) which deals with UK properties and does not make reference to TCGA 1992, s. 241A. This looks like an oversight but is still a concern.

In the rare scenario of a limited company operating an FHL business but with the properties themselves owned outside of the company, the associated disposal rules would apply on a sale; a 10 per cent tax rate is thereby still available subject to all the requirements of the legislation being met. In this regard care is needed in respect of TCGA 1992, s. 169P, which imposes restrictions on entitlement to entrepreneurs' relief where there have been changes in the use of the property during the period of ownership.

Such considerations do not apply where there have been changes in the usage of the asset for personal ownership either through a sole trader business or a partnership or indeed even where the life tenant of the trust is involved. In that case it is only necessary to meet the one year qualifying period. For such a disposal it is also worth considering the position where a property is in mixed use – with part being used for the purposes of the FHL business and part for another purpose such as a main residence or a long term let property. In accordance with TCGA 1992, s. 169L, entrepreneurs' relief applies to "assets used for the purposes of a business carried on by the individual or a partnership of which the individual is a member" and this is only restricted to the extent that there are excluded assets that are held as investments. As already mentioned, this is a difficult provision to interpret and it could apply in some circumstances. However, temporary letting of a property or letting of surplus property would not necessarily be considered as an "investment" and so would not necessarily be caught.

When dealing with the sale of a property, the ownership proportions for CGT purposes should be the same as those used in ITA 2007, s. 836 where there is jointly held property. However that section enables the profits of an FHL business to be apportioned between husband and wife or civil partners in whatever way the couple sees fit. Such an apportionment does not suggest that the property is not owned equally by the couple and so would not prevent both spouses or civil partners from being entitled to full entrepreneurs' relief. However, on a practical level it is probably safer to have a more even split in the 12 months prior to sale, just to remove any doubt as to entitlement to entrepreneurs' relief.

It is not possible to set an FHL loss against a capital gain under TCGA 1992, s. 261B as the loss is restricted. However, where it is considered that the business is carried on as a trade then that option would be available on any residual trading loss. However, it should be noted that in such a case relief is only being achieved on the trading loss at 10 per cent, so any loss relief option where a higher rate of relief can be achieved would be more desirable. In the same context, when planning a disposal, it is important to take into consideration capital losses, but where possible it would be better to relieve these at a higher capital gains tax rate than 10 per cent (but this will depend on the circumstances of the owners concerned).

6.3 Whole or part of the business

As explained above, entrepreneurs' relief is only available to an individual currently operating an FHL business where there is a sale of the "whole or part of a business". What does that mean in the context of furnished holiday lettings?

The term "whole or part of a business" was used in the former retirement relief legislation and a body of case law built up around the meaning of that term. Most of these cases concerned farmers and whether the sale of farmland and buildings amounted to a mere sale of assets or to a sale of part of the farming business. The taxpayer was unsuccessful in many of those cases and so it should not be rashly assumed that entrepreneurs' relief will be available without a careful review of the facts.

In the context of FHLs, the first stage is to determine the business concerned. This is the theme that we return to again and again throughout this book and the reader will appreciate that there are conflicting objectives for different taxes. Separation of businesses is beneficial for entrepreneurs' relief purposes as far as the "whole or part of a business" is concerned: if separate properties are regarded as separate businesses then there can be no doubt about the availability of entrepreneurs' relief on the sale of a property. This is consistent with mitigating VAT, where disaggregation of businesses is likely to be beneficial in most cases, but runs contrary to the objectives for inheritance tax planning purposes, where it is likely to be necessary to show that all of the activities amount to a single composite business.

Further, there are many different types of owners of FHL properties and the approach to the meaning of "whole or part of a business" will be different for farmers, hotel owners and bed and breakfast operators, who also undertake FHLs, as compared to someone who merely operates furnished holiday lettings.

In general, an operator of a single FHL business of, say, six units who sells one of those units is not going to be able to show that that is the sale of a whole or part of the business, assuming that he or she continues to operate the other units as part of the continuing complex. If it was the sale of one unit in the complex and the other five units were sold at or around the same time to different purchasers, as part of a method of disposing of the business, then in that scenario it should be possible to get the disposal to qualify. Clearly timing would be crucial and it would probably be better to have the business ceasing to operate before the sale takes place.

Conversely, an individual who operates a number of FHL properties, perhaps let through an agency, around different geographical locations, should be able to show that the sale of one property is the sale of a "whole or part of the business". However, to do this it would be necessary to show on the facts that the properties amounted to separate, distinct and clearly identifiable parts of the overall FHL activity. If different agents were used for the lettings, or if there were clearly separate and distinct factors in each area, there would then be a good argument that the sale of the property was a sale of part of the business. For properties in different EAA states, there is again a clear argument that this is the case.

There is guidance in the HMRC Capital Gains Manual at 64015 as follows:

> "Someone may own two shops in different towns and sell one of them, but continue with the other. Whether or not this amounts to the disposal of the whole or part of the business depends on the facts. The trader may be able to show that entirely separate businesses, connected only by common ownership, were conducted from each shop. Another possibility is that the activities of each shop, whilst contributing to a single business, form a separate, distinct and clearly identifiable part of the trade.

> For example, one shop may have been an outlet dealing exclusively with wholesale customers whilst the other was used only for retail purposes. Whether there are one or two separate businesses is a question of fact and guidance to help determine the matter can be found in the Business Income Manual at BIM 20050+."

If very similar properties are let in each location, there is considerable overlap of the type of guests staying in them and the properties are very much run as one activity, then it may be hard to show that the sale of one of them would be the sale of part of a business. However, if the properties are of a different size – say, a two bed property in one location has been sold whereas the other properties operated are four, five or six bedded properties – and it can be clearly shown that the clientele is different and the marketing and advertising approach is different, then entrepreneurs' relief should be available. It is a tricky area and it is important that good and comprehensive disclosure is made in the tax return.

6.4 Rollover relief

The business asset roll-over relief legislation in TCGA 1992, s. 152 to 157 is extended to apply to furnished holiday lettings by virtue of TCGA 1992, s. 241 and 241A. The capital gains tax legislation adopts the definitions used for income tax and corporation tax purposes as set out in the relevant acts.

The later subsections of s. 241 and 241A deal with computational provisions and matters of apportionment for all the CGT provisions to which the furnished holiday letting regime is applied (rollover relief, gifts of business assets, entrepreneurs' relief, relief for loans to traders and substantial shareholdings exemption). Sections 241(4) and 241A(6) provide that where the capital gains tax legislation is deemed to apply to the FHL activity, then the accommodation is taken to be used for those purposes for the entire period. So where an FHL activity is carried on it is not necessary to look at the relevant years of assessment or chargeable periods on a month by month basis so as to break down the activity between FHLs and other use of the property.

However, it may well still be necessary to consider the usage of the property over a longer period of time where the period of ownership includes activities other than FHLs. Further, s. 241(7) and 241A(9) deal with the possibility that only part of the property may be used for FHLs and such necessary adjustments as are required must be made on a just and reasonable basis. However, where a property is not let commercially as a furnished holiday letting due to works of construction or repair then this is still considered to be a time of qualifying activity.

The usage of a property is relevant when applying TCGA 1992, s. 152, in particular subsections 5 and 7 which provide that appropriate adjustments have to be made in certain circumstances. This will apply where an asset has not been used for the purposes of the trade throughout the entire period of ownership or where part of an asset has been used for the trade and part has not; for CGT purposes separate notional assets are created.

Example – roll-over and non-qualifying use of building

Kate inherits a family holiday home in September 2001. At the time of acquisition it is worth £250,000. It is used as a family holiday home for three years but is then let as a qualifying furnished holiday letting from September 2004. The property is sold in September 2011 for £400,000 and the proceeds are reinvested in another qualifying business activity.

The gain arising is £150,000. However as the property has only been let as furnished holiday letting accommodation for seven out of the ten years, only 70 per cent of the gain is eligible for roll-over relief, being £105,000.

In this example, it is not necessary for Kate to be operating the property as a furnished holiday letting at the time of sale in order to qualify for roll-over relief: the restricted apportioned roll-over relief would still be available to Kate if she had carried on the FHL activity for the first seven years and used it as a family holiday home for the final three years. It is therefore necessary to question clients closely in order to establish whether there is an historic FHL use of a property during the period of ownership (but only after 1982) if there is a possibility that the monies may be reinvested.

As mentioned above, apportionments may also be required where only part of the property has been used for an FHL activity and part for a non-qualifying activity. The most common scenario in which there is only partial use of a property is where there is owner's occupation included with the property, such that main residence relief under TCGA 1992, s. 222 would be available to exempt that element of the gain. However, there are other circumstances in which there could be a taxable non-qualifying use, such as where there are four units in a property and three are used as FHLs with the fourth being let as an assured short-hold tenancy to a long-term tenant. It is also perfectly conceivable that there could be a disposal of a property that has had partial usage as a furnished holiday lettings both over time and as a proportion of the building concerned.

Where it is intended to acquire an FHL property with the intention of rolling over another gain into it, TCGA 1992, s. 152(1) requires the new property to be taken into use for furnished holiday lettings on acquisition. The statutory language is restrictive and so there is an historic concessionary practice to allow a delay in an asset being taken into use where works of a capital nature are undertaken immediately on acquisition, as long as the asset is then used for the purposes of the qualifying trade immediately following the completion of those capital works. In the case of FHLs, it is certainly very normal for building works to be undertaken on the acquisition of a property but this point needs to be looked at carefully when advising clients on rolling over a gain into such a newly acquired property. It is important to avoid any unfortunate gaps that could otherwise occur and to make sure that the steps have been actively undertaken in connection with the FHL activity during the period of the building work.

Although it is necessary for a property to be taken into immediate use on acquisition, there is no clawback of the rollover relief given where the property subsequently ceases to be used for the qualifying activity. An historic planning approach to obtaining the benefit of roll-over relief for clients looking to invest in residential property has been for the individual concerned to acquire a property which is then used as a qualifying furnished holiday let for a period of time. This can subsequently be changed to being let on a long-term basis to an assured short-hold tenant. The point here is that the gain being reinvested into the FHL business does not have to arise from furnished holiday lettings but could be the reinvestment of a gain from another business activity such that the payment of capital gains tax is avoided. Such planning could equally well be applied to a company situation but it is more commonly encountered with individuals.

Example – rollover relief planning

George sells an unincorporated business for £500,000. Of this figure, £50,000 relates to goodwill and £450,000 to a property. The base cost of the goodwill is £35,000 whilst the base cost of the property is only £50,000.

George wants to invest the proceeds in property and receive rental income which he feels will be a secure form of retirement income. George's wife Mildred has only a very small amount of income (about £3,000) whereas George has about £10,000 of pension income. Both are over 65.

George does not want to pay any capital gains tax now as he feels it will erode the money he has available to invest (even at 10 per cent). George and Mildred live near Bournemouth.

George could reinvest £450,000 in a furnished holiday lettings business (one or more properties) such that rollover relief applies. After a year or so he could cease to holiday let the properties and let them on a long-term basis. Whilst he would have to acquire the properties in his own name, subsequent to the purchase, and meeting the rollover requirements, he could transfer half of the property (or properties) to Mildred to improve the income tax efficiency of the arrangements.

There would be no need to roll over the gain on the goodwill, which can be used to absorb George's annual exemption.

A final point to watch out for in respect of rollover relief and FHLs is contained in TCGA 1992, s. 241(6). This considers the situation whereby a claim for main residence relief is being made on a property that has been used as for furnished holiday letting on acquisition and on which a rollover relief claim was made at the time. The effect of the provision is to restrict the main residence relief under TCGA 1992, s. 222 from applying to the element of the gain increased by the previous rollover relief claim.

Example – effect of TCGA 1992, s. 241(6)

Matt bought a furnished holiday let in September 2001 for £250,000. At the time of acquisition a gain of £100,000 was rolled over into this giving a net base cost of £150,000.

The property was let as an FHL property from acquisition until September 2008. At that time Matt moved into the property and occupied it as his only or main residence until sale in September 2011. The property was sold in September 2011 for £400,000.

The gain arising is £250,000. The gain eligible for main residence relief is 30 per cent i.e. three years out of the ten years of ownership. However the effect of s. 241(6) is that that 30 per cent is applied not to the gain of £250,000 but to the gain that would have applied in the absence of the rollover relief claim of £150,000. Therefore the reduction of the gain by virtue of main residence relief is 30% x £150,000 = £45,000 leaving a chargeable gain of £205,000.

6.5   Owner occupation of the property

Whilst qualification for entrepreneurs' relief is beneficial, it only secures a 10 per cent tax rate such that there is still a liability to capital gains tax. By contrast, there is a possibility of absolute relief (in whole or part) where there has been owner occupation of the property and TCGA 1992, s. 222 main residence relief applies. This can either be on the facts that the property was at some point occupied as the main residence, or more usually by reason of election under s. 222(5). The benefits of main residence relief are not only in the period of time exempted, but also by reason of the extension to the final 36 months of deemed occupancy under s. 223(1) and by let property relief under s. 223(4).

The rules for deemed periods of occupancy provide scope for some very generous tax relief. In particular, once a property has qualified as a main residence then the final 36 months of ownership are automatically exempted for CGT purposes. Therefore, if two residences are available to the same person, and both at some stage qualified as an individual's main residence, the final 36 months of ownership for both properties will be exempt. Given that it is the "quality" as opposed to the "quantity" that determines occupation, a relatively short period of occupancy, say two to three months, can then entitle the owner to relief on the final 36 months as well as bringing let property relief into play.

Where a taxpayer has more than one residence (and there has been actual occupation of both), he or she needs to nominate which is to be regarded as the main residence. This should be done in writing to HMRC within two years of acquiring the second residence. This election may then be varied at a later date. Once the election is in place, the variation can be made without the need for the actual occupancy of the properties to change. Married couples or civil partners who live together can only have one residence that qualifies as their main residence (TCGA 1992, s. 222(6)). The HMRC Capital Gains Manual at 64512 contains an example where an election for a one-week period is shown as being acceptable.

Following the decision in *Griffin v Craig-Harvey*, it is generally accepted that an initial election must be made within two years of a taxpayer acquiring a second residence. If an election has not been made within two years, the option ceases to be available until a new combination of residences is acquired. Although it is commonly thought that a main residence election must be made whilst the two properties are still owned, an example in the HMRC Capital Gains Manual at 64512 shows an election being made after the sale of the property.

It should be noted that the requirement is to have two or more residences and this is different from ownership. While a property is let it cannot be occupied as a residence by the owner. Whilst this position is quite clear cut as far as properties let on assured short-hold tenancies are concerned, the position is more debatable on properties used as holiday accommodation. A temporary interruption in residence to let someone else occupy a property would be unlikely to amount to a loss of residency rights, but conversely where a property has been used for furnished holiday lettings for a considerable period of time with no family usage then this would be similar to the position of a long term let property and so a period of actual occupancy by the family could then suffice.

In the absence of an election there is a list of criteria in the HMRC Capital Gains Manual at 64552 to determine which of two or more residences is a person's main residence. The list includes looking at the address shown on tax returns, the address shown on third party correspondence, how each property is furnished, where the property owner is registered to vote, where the property is in relation to the person's place of work and where the owner's family stays. The HMRC Capital Gains Manual does say that the relative extent to which each residence is occupied is not a material factor.

In a case where no election has been made, and one is trying to determine the position on the facts, reference to the tests that are applied for council tax purposes to determine a main residence may be a possible guide. These are understood to be as follows:

1. **Occupation rights**
   a. At each residence review whether the individual is an owner, a tenant (and the nature of any tenancy), or a lodger of any accommodation provided with employment.
   b. What is his/her right to occupy a property?
   c. Is residence conditional? For example, dependent on holding a work permit.

2. **Personal connections**

   a. At which residence is the individual registered with a doctor or dentist?
   b. Where are the majority of his or her possessions kept?
   c. Where does he or she return to during periods of leave or at the end of employment?
   d. What are the long-term intentions?
   e. Where is the individual registered to vote?
   f. Consider the membership of clubs and other social activities.
   g. Which address is used as the usual postal address?
   h. Which property does he or she regard as the main residence?
   i. How is time split between the residences?

3. **Family connections**

   a. At which residence do the spouse and any dependents live?
   b. From which residence do any children attend school?
   c. At which residence does the individual spend time with the family?

4. **Other sundry issues**

   a. Merchant seamen are not considered to be resident on a ship.
   b. Services personnel are considered as mainly resident in accommodation, provided privately, rather than any service accommodation.

Where an FHL property has been owner-occupied, such that main private residence relief applies, let property relief should also apply. This is available where the dwelling-house or any part of it has been let as residential accommodation at any time during the period of ownership.

The capital gain arising attributable to the period of letting is chargeable only to the extent that it exceeds the lower of:

   a. the amount of the main residence relief;
   b. the capital gain arising during the let period; and
   c. £40,000.

The relief cannot give rise to an allowable loss. The limit of £40,000 is available to each property owner so a husband and wife (or both civil partners) owning a property can jointly claim a maximum of £80,000.

The definition of residential accommodation was examined in *Owen v Elliott* concerning a small hotel. During the summer season visitors stayed for short periods, but in the winter they often stayed for several months. In the summer, Mr Owen and his family lived in an annexe, but in the winter they occupied the whole hotel. On the disposal of the property, Mr Owen agreed with the Inspector of Taxes that one third of the gain on disposal was exempt under TCGA 1992, s. 222. Mr Owen then claimed further relief under the let property exemption, because he argued that he had provided residential accommodation in his private residence for the guests. HMRC argued that, in their view, providing accommodation for hotel guests was not letting the property as residential accommodation.

However, it was held that the let property exemption applied where property was "let . . . as residential accommodation". The phrase did not merely refer to premises let which were likely to be occupied as a home. Thus the lettings were within the definition of "residential accommodation" and further relief under TCGA 1992, s. 223(4) was available.

The view of HMRC on entitlement to let property relief is set out in Statement of Practice 14/80.

Cases: *Owen v Elliott (HMIT)* [1990] BTC 323; *Griffin v Craig-Harvey* [1994] BTC 3

6.6 Substantial shareholdings exemption

For the purposes of applying the substantial shareholdings exemption in TCGA 1992 Sch. 7AC, the term trade is extended to include the commercial letting of furnished holiday accommodation.

Law: TCGA 1992, s. 241, 241A

6.7 Irrecoverable loan to a furnished holiday lettings company

The definition of trade in TCGA 1992, s. 253 is extended to include the commercial letting of furnished holiday accommodation. The definition of commercial letting and furnished holiday accommodation is that used for income tax and corporation tax purposes, and so includes the letting of property in the EEA. However, it is important to note that s. 253 requires that the borrower (the company) must be resident in the UK.

This restriction to UK resident companies only is both surprising and particularly difficult to understand in the context of FHLs, given the extension to properties within the EEA. There must be an argument that this restriction is in breach of EU rules and that a protective capital loss claim should be considered if a loan is made to a non-resident company carrying on the commercial letting of FHL accommodation within the EEA.

Law: TCGA 1992, s. 241, 241A

6.8 Fixtures and fittings

In the context of considering the sale of a furnished holiday letting property it is important to remember the need to make an apportionment as between the freehold and leasehold property which is subject to capital gains tax and the fixtures and fittings and plant and machinery which will be dealt with within the capital allowances regime for income tax or corporation tax purposes. However, a claim for capital allowances on fixtures in the property (including integral features) does not reduce the base cost of the property when calculating a capital gain (TCGA 1992, s. 41(1)), though a fixtures claim may reduce the amount of any capital loss.

As considered in **Chapter 5**, substantial claims to capital allowances may be available on a newly acquired or newly refurbished FHL property. Where such capital allowances arise in respect of fixtures, it may well be that the capital allowances given are higher than the depreciation of the property at the time. As a result, on the sale of the property, it is likely that there will be a significant clawback of capital allowances previously given by means of a balancing charge.

For this reason some clients have been reluctant to make claims for capital allowances on fixtures and it is certainly worth considering the future potential income tax consequences of a sale before any claim for allowances is made. New purchasers will of course be interested in maximising their capital allowances claim on the acquisition of a property. For this reason, the vendor of an FHL property should not agree to an apportionment without fully understanding the implications but should always get appropriate advice prior to the signing of the contract.

A further possibility in respect of the fixtures is to enter into an election under CAA 2001, s. 198 to fix the value of the fixtures for tax purposes as between the seller and the purchaser. This election determines the proceeds to be used in the capital allowances computation and so can prevent a claw back of allowances in respect of integral features.

An election under s. 198 election can enable the owner of an FHL property to make a claim in respect of integral features and then to sell the property with capital allowance disposal proceeds of just £1 such that the full benefit of the capital allowances is retained by the seller. Such planning has recently started to be frowned upon by HMRC and it is likely that new legislation will be introduced to restrict such tax planning. There is existing anti-avoidance legislation in CAA 2001, s. 197 and it is likely that this will be strengthened or otherwise that restrictions will be imposed on the minimum figure that can be used in a s. 198 election.

7. Death and succession planning

7.1 Introduction

Furnished holiday lettings are often owned by families for very long periods of time and can have different uses over that period of ownership. For the families concerned, succession planning is often the number one issue, with the result that inheritance tax and capital gains tax are the most important taxes to be considered.

As far as inheritance tax is concerned, the availability of business property relief is the most significant consideration. This may in turn open up CGT planning opportunities, including the availability of hold-over relief, as it increases the options for the use of trusts. Even if inheritance tax is not an issue, perhaps because reliance has been placed on seven year survival with a potentially exempt transfer, CGT hold-over relief under TCGA 1992, s. 165 may still be an important consideration. This chapter examines these issues and deals in detail with the availability of business property relief and hold-over relief.

7.2 Business property relief

It is sensible to start by considering the application of business property relief to property letting generally. IHTA 1984, s. 105 is not reliant upon the definition of FHLs within ITTOIA 2005, but rather on the definition of whether or not the activity amounts to a non-investment business.

As explained in **Chapter 3**, MPs put forward amendments, during both the Finance Bill Committee debate in 1984 and the subsequent Report stage debate, for the FHL rules to apply to capital transfer tax as if furnished holiday lettings were a trade. These amendments were resisted by the government of the day. In the Report stage debate, at the final conclusion of two years or so of concern and discussion over this issue, the Chief Secretary to the Treasury, Peter Rees, summarised the government position as follows:

> "The whole problem was triggered by income tax – it had nothing to do with capital transfer tax. Although I accept that there may be a case – I do not go further than that – for giving capital transfer tax relief for such lettings that would take the debate into a new area."

Despite the suggestion that the matter might be returned to at a later date, that has not happened. Even with the furore of the April 2009 Budget proposal and subsequent debate there was no likelihood of the FA 2011 changes extending the rules to apply to business property relief.

The background to this issue is that claims for business property relief on let property have always been resisted by HMRC. Statements made by the Chief Secretary to the Treasury during the passage of the Finance Bill in 1976, which introduced the current business property relief legislation, made it clear that it was not intended to extend to landlords. This principle was followed by the Special Commissioners in *Martin v IRC* and *Burkinyoung v IRC*.

Therefore, whilst business property relief is a relief for businesses, the legislation does not extend it to activities that are principally an investment business. However, this is dealt with in the negative and IHTA 1984, s. 105(3) reads:

> "A business or interest in a business, or shares in or securities of a company, are not relevant business property if the business or, as the case may be, the business carried on by the company consists wholly or mainly of one or more of the following, that is to say, dealing in securities, stocks or shares, land or buildings or making or holding investments."

In *Hall and Hall* and in *Powell and Anor*, the issue was the application of this "wholly or mainly" rule in s. 105(3) in cases involving caravan parks. Both cases were lost by the taxpayers, on the grounds that the businesses were wholly or mainly investment because the trading sides of the businesses amounted to much less than 50 per cent of the whole. The subsequent caravan case of *George* was won by the taxpayer in the Court of Appeal on the grounds that the finding of fact by the Special Commissioner was reasonable. The holding of property as an investment was only one component of the business, and on the findings of the Special Commissioner it was not the main component. It was held that an active family business should not be excluded from business property relief, merely because a necessary component of its profit-making activity is the use of land.

In *George*, Carnwath L J acknowledged that caravan parks are particularly difficult to distinguish as between "investment" and "non-investment" as they are hybrid businesses. For instance, maintenance of the amenity areas of a caravan park is partly to maintain the investment, but is also part of the service provided to the residential occupiers. He also concluded that merely because services or facilities are required by the terms of a lease, and their cost is included in the rent, that does not cause them to lose their character as services. Subsequent judicial comment on the caravan cases in *Farmer* also highlighted the long term nature of the caravan lettings which were more in the nature of ground rents than short term accommodation. Short term letting is good for business property relief whilst long term letting is bad.

The cases of *Furness* and of *Weston* established that the courts will examine the matter "in the round", that is not looking merely at the turnover or profit produced by the investment side of a business relative to the trading activities. The respective capital values of the underlying assets, together with the time spent by both the proprietors and the employees on the two sides of the business, also have to be considered. All these tests then featured in the *Farmer* case in 1999.

The Special Commissioner's decision in *Farmer* was a significant milestone. It concerned an individual who died leaving a large farm with many properties which were let to third parties, because they were surplus to requirements. The thrust of the case was not just to look at the five relevant factors individually – the context of the business, the capital employed, the time spent, the turnover and the profits – but to consider the whole business "in the round". On the basis of the decision in *Farmer*, it is possible to argue that the overall activities amount to a business in totality. As already mentioned, the short term nature of the lettings was a key factor, but so also was the fact that the majority of the acreage was farmed. The historical context of the estate was also very influential.

The business was predominantly one of farming rather than a land and property business.

In the *Farmer* case there were 449 acres in total, including 22 tenancies not qualifying for agricultural property relief. Six of these were of original farm cottages; four were of original farm buildings or barns converted for use by small businesses; four were of original farm buildings used for storage; three were of mobile homes; two were of stable blocks, one of which was let with some grazing land; one was of a staff bungalow which was let with some stables and grazing land; one was of a prefabricated bungalow built by the deceased; and one was of redundant land for the storage of timber. The plan of the farm in the case showed that the buildings which were let were grouped in two main clusters towards the centre of the estate and the grazing areas which were let were contiguous to the clusters of let buildings.

It is worth considering in detail the short term nature of the lettings. Most of the residential lettings were short-hold tenancies for either six months or one year; the other lettings were either by licence, letter or leases for one year which were excluded from the provisions of the *Landlord and Tenant Act* 1954. There was one licence of a converted barn for commercial use which was, exceptionally, for five years; this longer term of tenancy was granted because, although the deceased had provided the materials for the conversion, the tenants had provided the labour to produce a purpose-built gymnasium and so a longer licence than usual had been granted in recognition of this. There were no FHLs in the case – which could only have strengthened a claim for business property relief.

The principle of considering the nature of the activities of the business "in the round" was further developed in the *Balfour* case. This concerned an estate that comprised 772 hectares (1,907 acres) of in hand and let farms as well as policy parks, woodlands and sporting rights, 26 let houses and two sets of business premises. The case was complicated by the historic ownership arrangements but the relevant point for these purposes is that the Upper Tribunal upheld the finding of facts of the First-tier Tribunal that these activities represented a single composite business that was mainly a trading activity. It reiterated the principles established in *Farmer* except that in *Balfour* the farming activities were smaller and it was not necessary for all of the activities to be carried on within the same entity (in *Balfour* there was both a trust and a partnership undertaking the activities). The key aspects were the historic connection between the properties as a single estate and the short term nature of the lettings.

A further point is whether the position is different for activities carried on by companies rather than by individuals. It has long been felt that companies are potentially in a stronger position. It was confirmed by *American Leaf Blending*, that "any gainful use to which [a company] puts any of its assets *prima facie* amounts to the carrying on of a business". Therefore, a portfolio of quoted investments held by a company will normally represent an investment business conducted by it, and so long as this is not the main business of the company, business property relief will be due on the whole value of the company.

There is a useful summary of the law in this area in *Land Management Ltd*. In this case, a company owned and let a freehold residential property, held and received dividends from shares in various companies, made an interest-bearing loan to a connected company, and received interest on a bank deposit. The Special Commissioner held that each of its activities, and all four in combination, amounted to carrying on business. As a result, it is possible to have an investment activity together with an otherwise trading company so that in total the combined activities amount to an overall business. However, this is the same as the position established by the *Farmer* and *Balfour* cases.

These cases are relevant to FHLs to the extent of trying to establish the boundary between investment and non-investment businesses. In general, the issue is the extent to which services are provided, and that is considered further below. However, the cases are much more pertinent to scenarios where FHLs are carried on as part of a wider business – most typically involving farming or an hotel. In such circumstances, the strongest case will be achieved where the activities are all within the same ownership, although the *Balfour* case provides support for looking at activities in different ownership as long as all of the activities, including the furnished holiday lettings, are managed as one business. The other key conditions are that the properties have an historic connection that ties them together and that they are all managed as one estate.

In addition to the cases considered above, the case law on trading versus property businesses considered in **Chapter 2** is also relevant and reference should be made to those cases as appropriate. Reference to the points on structuring of an FHL business in **Chapters 5** and **8** are also pertinent. Any advice on structuring should include consideration of business property relief and the case law above should be referred to.

Cases: *American Leaf Blending Co Sdn. Bhd. v Director-General of Inland Revenue* [1978] 3 All ER 1185; *Martin (Moore's Executors) v IRC* (1995) Sp C 2; *C J Burkinyoung (Exor. of Burkinyoung dec'd) v IRC* (1995) Sp C 3; *Hall (Exors of Hall dec'd) v IRC* (1997) Sp C 114; *Powell and Anor (Executors of Pearce dec'd) v IRC* (1997) Sp C 120; *Farmer & Anor (Exors of Frederick Farmer dec'd) v IRC* (1999) Sp C 216; *Furness v IRC* (1999) Sp C 202; *Weston v IRC* (1999) Sp C 222; *Land Management Ltd v Fox (HMIT)* (2002) Sp C 306; *IRC v George & Anor (Executors of Stedman Deceased)* [2003] BTC 8037; *HMRC v A M Brander as Exec of the Will of the late fourth Earl of Balfour* [2010] UKUT 300 (TCC)

7.3 Provision of additional services to achieve business property relief

In many cases the taxpayer will have an uphill struggle where the business is essentially that of letting property. Significantly, ITTOIA 2005, s. 322 does not extend to inheritance tax, as it applies to income tax and to most CGT reliefs, the deemed trading treatment of furnished holiday letting. The Inheritance Tax Manual used to state (at 25278) that business property relief would be allowed on even a single property used for FHLs provided that these were short-term and that the owner, whether himself or through an agent, was substantially involved with the holidaymakers in terms of their activities on and from the premises. This was the case even if the lettings were for part of the year only.

However, HMRC announced late in 2008 that they had been advised that their previous practice as set out above was incorrect in law. As such, it has been replaced by an approach which looks "more closely at the level and type of services rather than who provided them". The Inheritance Tax Manual at 25278 now states:

"In the past, we have thought that business property relief would normally be available where:

- the lettings were short term; and
- the owner, either himself or through an agent such as a relative, was substantially involved with the holiday makers in terms of their activities on and from the premises.

Recent advice from Solicitor's Office has caused us to reconsider our approach and it may well be that some cases that might have previously qualified should not have done so. In particular, we will be looking more closely at the level and type of services, rather than who provided them.

Until further notice any case involving a claim for business property relief on a holiday let should be referred to the Technical Team (Litigation) for consideration at an early stage."

The reference to "the level and type of services" implies that the assessment is closer to that of whether or not a trade is being carried on than the traditional definition of business. Anyone looking to argue this point in the near future should carefully consider that. Also, the comments go beyond holiday cottages and complexes and extend to other facilities including self-service hotels.

To qualify for business property relief it is necessary to show that the activity amounts to a business. This is a wider status than trade. The legislation in IHTA 1984, s. 105 requires only that the activity amounts to a business that is not "wholly or mainly ... making or holding investments". Whilst there has been no change in the tax law on this point, HMRC are trying to restrict claims for relief and are hoping to win a test case to dissuade future claims. Regardless of the legislative requirements, historically HMRC have tended to look at the level and type of services offered. The nature of services relevant to the claim include:

- provision of laundry;
- organisation of car hire;
- equipment rental;
- booking restaurants;
- cleaning and laundry services;
- providing food for the fridge or freezer; and
- the provision of swimming pools and games rooms.

The success of a claim may well depend upon the extent to which the owners - or their agent(s) – interact with the guests. In other words, is a holiday being provided or just accommodation?

Unlike the treatment for trading taxes, HMRC do not depend on the prescribed rules, but are more inclined to investigate each case, so there is much less certainty. To maximise the chances of success, the agreement between the owner and the holidaymaker should set out in detail the services on offer, and there should be documentary evidence of their availability and perhaps also their take-up (although that would be down to the holidaymakers). Services would obviously include the supply of linen and laundry; cleaning of the property perhaps during the week as well as at the end of the week; services such as gas, electricity and water; maintenance of the garden, and the disposal of rubbish. In addition there might be on offer the supply of groceries at the beginning of the let; shopping during the week; arranging for newspaper delivery and temporary membership of a sports club. It is understood that the supply of a landline telephone and a television is also thought important by HMRC.

Recent case law has confirmed the importance of considering the historical context of the business concerned. This point is considered further in the case law above. Where there is a long established FHL business then a court is likely to be more sympathetic to a claim for business property relief – especially in cases of farm diversification. It is therefore important to review the background to the business, and to enquire as to the status on the demise of any previous family owner, to see whether business property relief was achieved at that point in time.

It is also important to demonstrate active involvement of the owners: the provision of laundry services, cleaning services, welcome packs, food ordering arrangements, information on attractions and the provision of leisure facilities all help to take the business in the right direction away from being a passive investment activity. What is appropriate will depend upon the nature and the location of the business concerned. Particular events and attractions can help and the existence of a wedding licence is very helpful - the arrangements of such functions can be both good business, and very persuasive to HMRC.

There is no doubt that the current HMRC stance makes it very difficult to achieve business property relief on an individual property – especially if let through an agent and barely visited by an owner. Conversely there can be strong arguments in favour of larger complexes based on the criteria set out above. In between there are various shades of grey. The more hallmarks of a separate business the better, but reference should also be made to what has been said to HMRC for VAT purposes or to the local authority in respect of non-domestic rates. Such contemporaneous evidence, as to the intention and activities at the time, could be very persuasive at a later date.

7.4   Gifting a furnished holiday lettings property

Where the intention is to keep an FHL property within the family, there are a number of tax planning opportunities. This is because FHL properties that meet the qualifying criteria are able to benefit from TCGA 1992, s. 165 business asset hold-over relief, and they may also qualify for business property relief (see above), so enabling a gift into trust without a lifetime inheritance tax charge. In the latter case, hold-over relief under TCGA 1992, s. 260 would apply as it takes priority over s. 165.

Entitlement to s. 165 hold-over relief is extended to qualifying FHLs by TCGA 1992, s. 241 and 241A, both for individual properties and also for shares in an FHL company. In TCGA 1992, s. 165A(14), the meaning of "trade" is "subject to section 241(3)". It should be noted that the FA 2011 changes have not adjusted this to refer to section 241A as well. Potentially this means that a company owning and operating FHLs in the EEA does not qualify for hold-over relief under s. 165. Whilst care is clearly required on this point, such an interpretation is obviously contrary to intended government policy and would be discriminatory. Most likely this is an omission in drafting that will be corrected at a later date.

The attraction of s. 260 hold-over relief is that it does not have the restriction imposed by TCGA 1992, Sch. 7 which applies to s. 165 hold-over relief where it has not been used as a business asset throughout the entire period of ownership (or 1982, if later). It is important to remember that whilst for entrepreneurs' relief, it is only necessary to consider a one year qualifying period, the Sch. 7 restriction requires the entire period of ownership to be considered. For FHL properties it is very common for there to be non-business use during the period of ownership – usually long term letting on assured short-hold tenancies.

Sch. 7 requires that the FHL property usage is considered over the period of ownership (both in terms of sequential or co-terminous alternative usage). A restriction to the held-over gain is then applied using the formula A/B, where A is the number of days of business usage during the period of ownership and B is the total number of days in the period of ownership. It is also important to remember that the property must be a qualifying FHL at the time of the gift if it is to qualify for hold-over in the first place.

Where the FHLs are owned by a company, but there has been non-qualifying activity of some description, Sch. 7 imposes a restriction calculated on a different basis. In this scenario the formula CBA/CA is used, where CBA is Chargeable Business Assets and CA is Chargeable Assets. In such a case it is necessary in the first instance for the company concerned to qualify as the individual's personal company in accordance with TCGA 1992, s. 165(8). This is similar to the entrepreneurs' relief qualification but is less restrictive as it does not have the 5 per cent ordinary shares requirement (only the 5 per cent of the votes condition). However, with a company it is necessary to look at all of its activities rather than a property-by-property approach. So for the company it is necessary to assess whether there are substantial non-trading activities (the 20 per cent test).

In some cases, it may be appropriate to incorporate an FHL business as part of the succession arrangements. In such a case, TCGA 1992, s. 162 relief could apply as it is a business being incorporated, as an alternative to relying on the s. 165 hold-over relief. However, the most common approaches are either an outright gift of a property to a child or grandchild or a transfer to a trust. In the latter case, s. 260 would apply and the two key issues to address are the inheritance tax position and the potential restriction to main residence relief by virtue of TCGA 1992, s. 226A.

That section prevents main residence relief where the gain is one that has been postponed by hold-over relief under s. 260. It applies where there is the disposal of, or of an interest in, a private residence by an individual or the trustees of a settlement, where that disposal took place on or after 10 December 2003. It must also be shown that all or part of the gain arising on disposal would be exempt by the private residence provisions of TCGA 1992, s. 223 and that the allowable base cost expenditure was reduced following an earlier disposal (or disposals) for which a s. 260 hold-over relief claim was made. In this situation, no main residence relief will be available in relation to a later disposal. Therefore, this does not prevent the making of a claim for hold-over relief, but does prevent a future claim for main residence relief.

A good example of why this anti-avoidance provision was introduced is to consider an individual who had a family holiday home, which did not qualify for main residence relief. The individual transferred ownership of the property to a discretionary settlement that was not settlor-interested and made a claim under s. 260. Acting in accordance with the settlement deed, the trustees allowed a beneficiary, probably a close relative of the transferor, to occupy the property as a qualifying residence. When the occupation terminated, the property was then sold. As throughout the period of ownership by the trustees the property qualified as a private residence, the entire gain arising on disposal, including that held over by the earlier s. 260 claim, would have been exempt from tax. It is important to remember that where a business asset is transferred to a trust, there is not a choice as to which hold-over relief to use; rather, s. 260 takes priority such that this restriction bites.

Further, whilst we are concerned with FHLs rather than second homes, there is considerable overlap: many long-held family properties may be used as FHLs for a period before reverting to being used primarily by an extended family. Therefore, where trust ownership arrangements are being used for succession purposes it is vital to make the owners aware of this future restriction on the property. In many cases, there is a long-held family property and there is no intention of sale such that the limitation on main residence relief is irrelevant. Alternatively, where the main intention is to benefit a specific family member, who will in turn occupy the property as a second home, a gift under s. 165 outside of a trust structure may well be better, followed by an election under TCGA 1992, s. 222(5). In the context of any such advice, close questioning of the future intentions is vital, and the appropriate health warnings should be given.

There is a further (and separate) point to watch where advice is being given on the future sale of a property: it is important to ask detailed questions about the acquisition of a property in case it was acquired by a transfer from a trust after 10 December 2003.

The lifetime inheritance tax charge (at 20 per cent) may need to be considered if business property relief is not available. However, it will often be the case that the property (or share of a property) being transferred to the trust is less than the available nil rate bands of a married couple or civil partners. In terms of tax planning on succession, the fallback option of the available nil rate bands often enables the position on business property relief to be tested in circumstances where no actual tax payment will arise if the argument is lost.

7.5   Income tax issues to consider on the gift of a property

For income tax purposes a gift of a property may well be the cessation of an FHL business as far as the donor is concerned. This may have implications for payments on account for self-assessment tax purposes and also perhaps for net relevant earnings. The converse is likely to be true for the recipient, although it should also be borne in mind that the question of whether or not the business is a trade needs to be considered in the light of the personal circumstances of the owner rather than of the business in isolation. It is perfectly possible that it may be treated as furnished holiday lettings for tax purposes for one of the owners and as a trade for the other – either the donor or the recipient, as appropriate. Also, whilst for CGT purposes it is only necessary to consider the usage of the property in the hands of the donor as far as s. 165 hold-over is concerned, for other tax purposes it will be necessary to consider the position of both the donor and the recipient.

This will be especially true for capital allowances, particularly if a claim has been made in respect of fixtures. Whilst it is possible to transfer the plant and machinery assets at tax written down value under CAA 2001, s. 266 where the parties are connected under CAA 2001, s. 575 (which is likely to be the case in respect of a gift), this does assume that the successor will carry on the FHL business. If a gift is being made of an existing FHL business, but the recipient will use it either as a second home or as a long term letting property, then there will be a disposal of the plant and machinery for capital allowances purposes as far as the donor is concerned. Depending on the circumstances, this could lead to a large balancing charge.

8.   Other UK taxes

8.1   Introduction

There are a number of other UK taxes that owners of furnished holiday lettings may have to consider in the course of operating their business. However, these tax issues are not specific to FHLs and are not dependent upon the specific rules in ITTOIA 2005 and CTA 2009 in any way. However, to the extent that such tax issues do impact on the specific FHL rules, or that they give rise to very commonly encountered issues and problems, it is worth providing some commentary. These points are covered in this chapter.

8.2   Non-domestic rates

Local business taxation is another area that exposes the difficulty of the boundary between long term occupation of a domestic property and the letting of holiday accommodation. It is also a common source of grievance. During the period when abolition of the FHL rules was under consideration, owners would often complain that they did not see why they should be liable to non-domestic rates if the government felt that such businesses should be taxed as ordinary furnished lettings.

The position of local taxation is separate from that of the tax issues that rely on the special FHL rules, but it would be inappropriate to ignore this issue. There is clearly an overlap in the definition and purpose of all the tax rules on self-catering accommodation but it is unlikely that there will be any more joined up thinking on this point any time soon.

The history of local government taxation helps to explain the liability of self-catering accommodation to non-domestic rates. Prior to the changes introduced by the Thatcher administration in the 1980s, all properties in the UK were rated – domestic or otherwise. However, the abolition of rates by the repeal of the *General Rate Act* 1967 and the introduction of the community charge by the *Local Government Finance Act* 1988 required a new non-domestic rating system in England and Wales. Whilst the community charge was quickly abolished and replaced by the council tax this did not dispense with the non-domestic rating system and so it remained necessary to continue to distinguish between domestic and non-domestic property.

In England and Wales the treatment of domestic property is set out in the *Local Government Finance Act* 1988, s. 66. This covers the rating of self-catering accommodation in England and Wales. Different provisions apply to Scotland and Northern Ireland (and there are even some differences between the provisions applying between England and Wales).

The basic requirement in both England and Wales is that a property is not domestic if, in a year, it will be available for letting commercially, as self-contained accommodation, for short periods totalling 140 days or more. "Commercially" means on a commercial basis, and with a view to the realisation of profits (sub-section 8A). However, in Wales there is a further requirement that the accommodation must be actually let for 70 days in a year as well. No such provision applies in England.

Whilst these definitions clearly have their roots in the FA 1984 definition of furnished holiday lettings, the definition is separately contained in the legislation and so is in no way based on the legislation in ITTOIA 2005 or CTA 2009. As a result, any change in those statutes has no bearing on the position for non-domestic rates. Indeed, the position in Wales was only changed in 2010 by SI 2010/682 whilst the English position was established by the original statutory instrument in 1990 (SI 1990/162).

Non-domestic rates are calculated by estimating the annual rental value of the property based on its size, type and location. For furnished holiday lettings the annual profit generated by the property may well be the best basis for determining the value for rating purposes. However, any owners' accommodation should remain subject to council tax. The liability to non-domestic rates is tax deductible for income or corporation tax purposes.

In some cases a rates relief may be available, depending on the location of the property or the size and nature of the business. Specifically, agricultural land and buildings are exempt from non-domestic rates. In this context, the definition of an agricultural building provides that it cannot be a dwelling. So, agricultural dwellings are liable to either council tax or non-domestic rates.

Unoccupied dwellings can benefit from an exemption from council tax of up to six months. If there is expected to be a period of low (or no) occupancy of an FHL property then it may be better to try to have a property reclassified as domestic rather than commercial to take advantage of this and to avoid a liability to non-domestic rates. Where a property ceases to be intended to be let as self-catering accommodation then re-classification may be appropriate.

For council tax there can also be a relief for second homes where a local authority chooses to offer this; this could apply in a case where a family holiday home is also occasionally let to holidaymakers. However, such a property would not be expected to meet the FHL qualifying criteria (see **Chapter 3**).

There has been no suggestion to date that the criteria for non-domestic property will be changed to bring them into line with the increased day count limits from April 2012. Therefore, the possibility remains that a property could be liable to non-domestic rates and yet not achieve the FHL qualifying criteria. A further point is that, where reliance is being placed upon the period of grace, the genuine intention to let requirement would mean that the property should be subject to non-domestic rates.

8.3   VAT considerations

As with non-domestic rates, a common area of grievance for owners against the proposed abolition of the FHL rules was the VAT treatment of holiday accommodation as compared to the exempt status of property income generally. However, for VAT purposes, the FHL status of a property for ITTOIA 2005 or CTA 2009 is irrelevant. The VAT status of holiday accommodation income is derived from EU law and the relevant tests and conditions are entirely separate from those applying for direct tax purposes. A further point is that not all property income is exempt, so even that grievance is not entirely fair.

Whilst the VAT rules are entirely separate from the special furnished holiday lettings rules that are the subject of this book, that does not mean that it is right to entirely ignore them. The starting point is to consider how holiday accommodation is defined for VAT purposes. This is dealt with in VATA 1994, Sch. 9, Grp. 1, which defines the provision of accommodation by an hotel, inn, boarding house or similar establishment. It also separately defines holiday accommodation as to whether it is advertised or held out as holiday accommodation or whether it is suitable for holiday or leisure use.

Such income is standard rated by virtue of VATA 1994, Sch. 9 Grp. 1, Item 1(e) and an owner will be subject to compulsory registration if his or her total VAT-able supplies exceed the VAT registration threshold. Voluntary registration is otherwise possible and may be considered where there is an acquisition of a new property which is liable to VAT at the standard rate, on the refurbishment of holiday accommodation or on a business acquired as a TOGC where the vendor was VAT registered.

Whilst the letting of holiday accommodation is standard rated, the letting of a property during the off season could still be exempt. VAT Notice 709/3 explains at para. 5.5 that:

> "If you let your holiday accommodation during the off season, you may treat your supply as exempt from VAT provided:
>
> * it is let to a person as residential accommodation
> * it is let for more than 28 days and
> * holiday trade in the area is clearly seasonal."

The treatment of deposits for VAT can give rise to complications. This is particularly so where deposits are refundable, although the case of *Clowance plc* in respect of timeshare accommodation confirmed that deposits are taxable on receipt, regardless of the date of the holiday: the receipt of the deposit is a tax point. Another holiday accommodation case on the same issue was *Moonrakers Guest House* which again confirmed that the tax point was when the deposit was received, though if it was subsequently refunded to the holidaymaker, the output VAT could be adjusted at that time.

For those furnished holiday lettings businesses that are trading over the VAT threshold but under £150,000 there remains the option of the flat rate scheme. This scheme is of limited application to FHL accommodation, though it does depend on the individual circumstances. Most furnished holiday lettings businesses that trade close to the VAT threshold will try to restrict bookings to prevent exceeding the threshold slightly and suffering a substantial loss of income. VAT registered businesses will usually be those with a number of units, such that they substantially exceed the threshold. Therefore the turnover limits of the flat rate scheme provide a relatively small window for operators, though the ability to stay within the scheme with VAT inclusive income up to £230,000 is an advantage.

A further problem with the flat rate scheme is the lack of relief for input tax. This is unattractive to many FHL businesses that incur VAT on agency commission, repairs and small capital expenditure. The flat rate scheme is therefore more likely to appeal to owners who do not use an agency and do not incur much VAT on their repairs expenditure. For such businesses there may well be a particular short term opportunity to take advantage of the scheme when first required to register because of the 1 per cent discount in the first year.

Another important point to consider, though, is other business income of which the most commonly encountered in the context of furnished holiday lettings is rental income from non-FHL properties. This was considered in *ICAN Finance* which confirmed that the flat rate must still be applied to such income. This could give rise to a substantial VAT liability and so makes the scheme very unattractive in such circumstances.

It may be the case that, on acquisition, a newly constructed property will satisfy the criteria for the building to be a dwelling within VATA 1994, Sch. 8, Grp. 5, Item 1. In that case, it should still be a zero-rated supply at the time despite the fact that the purchaser may intend to use the property for holiday accommodation. It is the nature of the building and not the use that determines this. VATA 1994, Sch. 8, Grp. 5, Item 2 states that the zero rate applies to "the supply in the course of construction of a building designed as a dwelling or number of dwellings".

Therefore, as long as the building satisfies the tests for a dwelling, zero rating applies. Indeed, even the self-build scheme can apply, as confirmed in the case of *Jennings* and in R&C Brief 29/10. However, different rules apply if the property does not qualify as a dwelling, as a result of occupancy restrictions. The issue of occupancy restrictions was considered in *Barbara Ashworth*. The conclusion is that an occupancy restriction alone is not sufficient to turn a dwelling into holiday accommodation. The property must also amount to holiday accommodation on the facts in the first place. The definition of dwelling is considered in **Chapter 5**.

Tax planning to minimise VAT on the construction of new holiday accommodation was held to have succeeded in *Lower Mill Estate Ltd.* This concerned a planning scheme to supply a building plot (instead of the completed property) for a holiday home, with a separate building contract being entered into for the construction of the property. The supply of the plot remained standard rated, whereas the construction of the property was a zero rated supply. A further benefit of this planning was that there is an SDLT saving because of the reduction in the value of the initial supply (the value of the plot was much lower than the supply of a completed property). This case has wider significance than just for furnished holiday lettings and in *Lower Mill Estate Ltd* it specifically said that "a taxpayer who has alternative courses open to him is entitled to choose that which minimises his liability to VAT".

For large holiday accommodation providers there are definitely VAT issues to consider but, as has already been said, these are not specific to the furnished holiday lettings regime. They arise, rather, from the same complex issues that lie at the root of much of the conflict between business premises and dwellings. However, one issue that is of more relevance concerns business splitting and the desire to minimise VAT by keeping the turnover below the VAT threshold. Such planning may conflict with best advice on the optimum structuring from the furnished holiday lettings perspective as considered in **Chapters 2** and **7**. Therefore this specific issue is considered below.

Cases: *Barbara Ashworth v C&CE LON* 94/221A; *Lower Mill Estate Ltd v R&C Commissioners* [2009] UKFTT 38 (TC); *Jennings v HMRC* [2010] UKFTT 49 (TC), [2011] UKFTT 298 (TC); *ICAN Finance v HMRC* [2011] UKFTT 81 (TC); *Clowance plc* [1987] VTD 2541; *C&E Commissioners v Moonrakers Guest House Ltd* [1992] BTC 5077

8.4 Artificial separation of businesses

For most furnished holiday lettings, the income is below the VAT threshold on a standalone basis. However, if the FHL business is combined with other activities then the result can often be that the income from the activity becomes liable to VAT at the standard rate. So, there is an obvious financial desire to keep the income separate from the other activities by having different ownership of the businesses.

This issue is most commonly encountered with farms, bed and breakfasts and small hotels. Whilst the immediate financial attraction of separating the businesses is compelling, there are two important points to be aware of:

1. the ability of HMRC to make a direction under VATA 1994, Sch. 1, para. 1A that the businesses concerned should be jointly registered for VAT; and
2. that the separation of the activities may damage a future claim for business property relief for inheritance tax purposes or any argument for trading status.

In this context it is also important to remember that if the income is assessed as furnished holiday lettings and returned on that basis for income tax purposes (or conceivably corporation tax purposes) then that income remains property income. As such it is assessable on the owners of the property albeit with the ability to allocate the income between a married/civil partnership couple as they choose in accordance with ITA 2007, s. 836. So, if a farming partnership property is used for furnished holiday lettings, the income from it is part of the farm in the absence of any other arrangements and is partnership property business income. (This issue does not arise where a bed and breakfast is part of a farm as the bed and breakfast income is trading income as well.)

From a business property relief perspective, it is far better that all of the activities are maintained as an integral whole (see **Chapter 7**). Where advice is given to separate out businesses for income tax and VAT purposes, this downside should be highlighted.

Whether HMRC can issue a direction to combine supposedly separate businesses for VAT purposes has been the subject of case law including *Hundsdoerfer*, *Smith (t/a The Salmon Tail)*, *Trippitt* and *Forster & Anor*. Of these, HMRC was only successful in defending its decision in *Smith (t/a The Salmon Tail)* – a case which concerned the separation of a public house from food and accommodation. In that case, there was no payment from the food and accommodation business for use of the premises. This can be contrasted with *Trippitt* where Mr Trippitt ran both the pub and catering business and Mrs Trippitt carried on a bed and breakfast but with a commercial contribution for the use of the premises.

Hundsdoerfer concerned a farm and a bed and breakfast, as did *Forster.* In *Hundsdoerfer,* Mrs Hundsdoerfer paid rent for use of the premises to Mr Hundsdoerfer but that was not the case in *Forster.* Instead, in the latter case, there was the more troublesome finding that although the property used by Mrs Forster for the bed and breakfast was in the farming partnership accounts and was described as the "farmhouse" it no longer fulfilled that role and was considered to be a private domestic dwelling for these purposes. This cannot be helpful from the point of view of establishing agricultural property relief at a later date.

Two other points in *Forster* are worthy of note:

1. the arrangements were historic, as Mrs Forster had operated the bed and breakfast since 1975 when the composition of the farming partnership was very different; and
2. one of the factors HMRC considered was whether there had been any farm diversification grant, which there had not been in this case.

It is important that a proper assessment is made of the circumstances in each case and that all the tax issues are fully considered – both short and long term.

Cases: *Hundsdoerfer* [1990] (VAT TD 5450); *Smith (t/a The Salmon Tail)* [1999] (VAT TD 16190); *Trippitt* [2001] (VAT TD 17340); *Forster & Anor* [2011] UKFTT 469 (TC)

8.5   National Insurance and payroll taxes

The rules in ITTOIA 2005 do not apply for National Insurance purposes. As such, the income from furnished holiday lettings is not liable to Classes 2 and 4 NIC, unless it constitutes a trade, as it is rental income. In cases where an HMRC officer believes that the activities may amount to a trade (which is the reverse of what one might expect, in view of the loss relief position), a challenge may be received. Reference should be made to the analysis in **Chapter 2**. In any case many furnished holiday lettings owners are over state retirement age and so would have no liability to National Insurance.

One does come across complicated or contrived arrangements where the aim is to pass the income to someone other than the legal owner(s) of the property. These give rise to all kinds of problems and show a lack of understanding of the fact that such income remains land and property income for tax purposes. The concern here is that if a property is owned by, say, a mother and father but operated by a daughter who takes all the profits and declares them for tax purposes then what is the correct interpretation of the position?

If the mother and father declare the income but pass it to their daughter then that could be no more than a gift. However, if they do not declare the income for tax purposes and it is being returned by the daughter then what bearing does this have? It could be self-employment or employment income in the hands of the daughter – either of which would have National Insurance implications. Even then, it should have been returned by the parents with the expenditure shown. The only other possible interpretation is that the activity amounts to a trade which is solely operated by the daughter, such that it does not represent land and property income at all. This would be a challenging position to take up but if that is considered a reasonable possibility then reference should be made to the arguments put forward in **Chapter 2** as to trading status.

The danger with any such arrangement as this is that unwanted tax liabilities could arise. It is therefore incumbent upon any adviser to establish the ownership position of a property carefully before preparing accounts and returns.

Finally, where staff are engaged it is still necessary for the owner to consider the resulting PAYE obligations, including completion of forms P46 etc.

8.6   Working tax credits

The issue over whether furnished holiday lettings amount to trading activities rather than being property income is considered in **Chapter 2**. The issue permeates much of what is considered throughout this book. As well as the UK taxes already considered, this point is also relevant to entitlement to working tax credits.

Regulation 4 of the *Working Tax Credits (Entitlement and Maximum Rate) Regulations* 2002 provides in the fourth condition that "the number of hours which a person undertakes qualifying remunerative work is ... in the case of a person who is self-employed, the number of hours he normally performs for payment or in expectation of payment".

So, in order to have working hours for the purpose of working tax credits it is necessary to be self-employed. Elsewhere in reg. 4 there is also reference to "the profits of a trade, profession or vocation". Although that reference is not directly applicable to the scenario that would be considered in the case of furnished holiday lettings, it indicates the basis on which the draftsman was interpreting "work".

The problems over the drafting of the working tax credits rules are well known and it is no surprise that the peculiar status of furnished holiday lettings was not considered at the time that the rules were introduced. The correct interpretation of those rules is that hours spent in an FHL activity do not qualify for working tax credits, and so awards made on the basis of that activity are incorrect. If a limited company was involved then there would be no such problem as in that case it is only necessary for the individual to be employed and there is no restriction on the nature of the activities of the employer. Employment of one spouse or the other is also possible.

In various discussions with HMRC during the course of the consultation process the issue of working tax credits was raised and clarification and guidance on this issue was requested. However, at the time of writing nothing has yet been issued. Where the income and family circumstances are such that entitlement to working tax credits involves a substantial sum being due then this needs to be taken into account in the structuring of the furnished holiday lettings business activity. On a strict interpretation of the rules, it would seem that it is necessary for at least one of the couple to be employed in such circumstances in order to qualify. The importance of working tax credits in terms of business structuring is addressed in **Chapter 5**.

Table of legislation

Index of cases

General index

Printed and bound in Great Britain by
Marston Book Services Limited, Didcot